AGING SUDDENLY AT 83
(On the Hudson)

AGING SUDDENLY AT 83 (On the Hudson)

W. L. STAATS

ISBN-13: 9781541240070
ISBN-10: 1541240073

Dedication

To Uncle Will who kept the family together after dad died

Acknowledgements

A grateful thank you to Edith Leet, Niece Monica and Daughter Vicky who proof read the work. Most of all, thanks to my family and friends who unwittingly provided the content.

Table of Contents

Anxiety

AGING SUDDENLY AT 83 (on the Hudson)

One January morning I awakened to the realization that it was my 83rd birthday. All of the sudden *I Felt O-L-D* as in: ancient, withered, feeble, a relic, over-the hill–possibly even the target of an archeological dig. This was puzzling since no earlier birthdays ever had such a disturbing effect.

Why this dramatic change in attitude? I had been through scores of birthdays but never before felt the sudden impact of the advancing years. For some time I secretly prided myself that I was somewhat of a Ponce de Leon and had discovered the fountain of youth– right up until that damned day when I reached 83.

Perhaps the sheer magnitude of years of longevity finally caught up with me. Or, was it a delayed shocking reaction to a variety of influences including: (1) world events (2) family— past and present (3) health

(4) social life (5) formal education/career/travel (6) involvement in physical activity, and (7) spirituality.

I decided to comb through the past to solve the perplexing question of why, on this particular birthday, aging had become an overwhelming concern.

One

LANDMARK BIRTHDAYS

With time on my hands and no challenging commitments, I have spent hours and hours reflecting on the influences which could have brought about this newly-hatched panic over aging. I thought about those landmark birthdays of the adult years.

As their 30th birthdays approached I noticed considerable apprehension among my friends about reaching that age. Many dreaded what they foresaw as the end of youth and the beginning of a lifetime of responsibility. Not me! I look backward on those past youthful years as a time of endless uncertainties which bedeviled me. It seemed a time of apprehension over such problems as: Who to ask out for a date? How to get more money? Where to go to college? What occupation to choose? How to react in negative situations? There were endless problems and worries. By 30, much of that was behind me. I had served in the military, completed college, and had even married and started my family. I looked forward to the future.

Nor was the 40th birthday traumatic. I was one lucky dude. I loved my job and my family. My teaching career had taken an adventuresome turn when, for the first time, I became involved with computers. It was the cutting edge at the time and somehow I had taken the bold step to do something entirely different.

When my 50h birthday rolled around, I was broadsided by the reaction of a friend's eight year old son when I mentioned that it was my birthday.

"How old are you, Mr. Staats?" he asked. "Fifty!" I admitted.

"Holy cow! That's half a century!" he exclaimed. Putting it in those words seemed to make it a very long span of time.

I didn't dread 60, either. Hurdles with health problems were ahead but the fun of dealing with a family of seven growing children was an experience not to be missed. There was always excitement in our home--sometimes too much.

In my late 60s I had a serious bypass operation but was blessed with an extremely competent doctor, who also happened to be a woman with a great sense of humor.

By age 70, I was looking forward to the golden years of full-time retirement. I'd given up fulltime teaching when eligible for social security but had stayed on in an adjunct status. The time was approaching to cut ties with the college and to travel and to enjoy a life free from growing children and job responsibilities.

Not long after leaving the college, tragedy struck. I lost my life partner to ovarian cancer in the 47th year of our marriage. Faith and my extended family were my salvation in her last six months of agony and also during those empty days, weeks and months following the loss.

Age 80 was a great occasion for dinners and other celebrations. I reveled at reaching that landmark age. To me, it represented freedom to throw off the shackles of restraint. Freedom to do my own thing in terms of culinary preferences, apparel choices, and personal observations and behavior

To those who criticized my eating habits and/or attire, I frequently quoted Chapter 6 verse 25 from St. Matthew in the Holy Bible. "Therefore I say unto you, take no thought for your life, what ye shall eat, or what ye shall drink; nor yet for your body, what ye shall put on. Is not the life more than meat, and the body than raiment?" The quoting of scripture stopped the critics every time.

It was a time of freedom for me to make outlandish comments, which were often countermanded by someone apologetically saying, "Pay no attention to him. He's eighty, you know." This, of course, only encouraged me to make more and more bizarre statements once I was assured that I could get away with it.

Getting through scores of birthdays was just one factor affecting my apprehensions at reaching age 83. There were many other variables which played a role in my reaction—world events and family background, for instance.

Two

World Events

In my lifetime there have been several unforgetta-ble events which may have influenced my reaction to reaching age 83. Apparently, the solution is to deal with the trauma by relying upon resiliency nurtured by experience. Could there be a fear of some forth-coming disaster which would dramatically reshape my lifestyle–one with which coping would be impossible?

After all, I've lived through some occurrences which have been remarkable experiences for everyone who witnessed them.

Unforgettable Dates

December 7, 1941—Pearl Harbor Day

The shock of the Japanese attack on Pearl Harbor on December 7, 1941 is a vivid memory for me. I can so clearly recall being at the homestead with my family and several friends listening to the radio show, *The Inner Sanctum Mystery.* This was a Sunday tradition during the cold weather months. There were about a dozen of us in the room. It was late in the afternoon and darkness had closed in on this chilly December day. I was nine years old.

Suddenly the living room door burst open and in strode Howie Lout, a high school classmate of my brother Larry who would be graduating in six months. Howie was in a high state of agitation and nervously announced, "We've been attacked by Japan. It happened at Pearl Harbor, a military outpost at Hawaii."

The room went silent. No one could absorb the impact of such a profound world-shaking horror. Soon the radio had canceled the regular programming and the airwaves were full of the news.

Threats of war had been looming for years–not from Asia but from Europe where Adolph Hitler had subdued a number of adversaries and was in the process of annihilating England. President Roosevelt and Prime Minister Winston Churchill had developed a close relationship, with Churchill continuously urging the United States to join in the war effort. In this nation, however, there was an extremely powerful group of isolationists—*America First* zealots opposed to us getting involved in a world wide conflagration. It took the Japanese to goad the United States into action.

Our family was deeply affected by the war. My two oldest brothers, Larry and Kim, were at an age eligible for military service, and brother Barry was just a few years shy of eighteen. Practically every one of my two older brother's friends were eligible. Within two years, the full impact of the war was felt. The enthusiasm and camaraderie of youth disappeared from our Sunday gatherings.

Brother Kim was the first to go. He didn't need much impetus because he hated going to high school. As a matter of fact, because of disciplinary problems, mainly absenteeism, he was asked to leave the Rensselaer school system in his junior year and transfer to the new East Greenbush high school which was in a rural setting not far from Rensselaer.

The war was started on December 7. On December 8 brother Kim threw his bagged lunch into a ditch and, instead of going to school, headed for the Navy recruiting office. He was just shy of 18 and my mom had to sign papers for him to enlist at that young age. Tears flowed abundantly. After completing boot camp at Great Lakes training station in Chicago, Kim was assigned aboard a

Destroyer Escort (DE). Unfortunately, he was prone to seasickness and the rolling and pitching of the DE was more than he could endure.

Since sea surface duty was not an option, Kim was asked to make a choice–either get out of the Navy or transfer to the submarine service. He chose the latter and was stationed in the Pacific aboard the *USS WHALE*. He saw a lot of military action, but was most reluctant to talk about it once he returned home.

Brother Larry graduated from high school and then took a job as a machinist with the General Electric Corporation (GE) in Schenectady. He watched as his closest friends, one by one, joined the service. He, too, followed suit and, like brother Kim, did his training at the Great Lakes base. Following boot camp, Larry put in a request to become a Navy pilot and began his training as a cadet at Dartmouth College in New Hampshire. Within a few months, he became impatient, fearing that he would spend the entire war training to be a pilot. He deliberately lowered his grades so that he would be dropped from the program and reassigned. He got his wish. Within a few months, Larry was assigned to PT boat duty in the Pacific. He remained at this station in the Philippines for the duration of the war, but missed any military action.

Howie Lout, the friend who dramatically announced the start of World War II back in 1941, was the only acquaintance to be seriously injured. He and several other Marines entered a cave in which Japanese soldiers were reported to be ensconced. There was a detonation and several Marines were killed. Howie lost an eye and suffered a severely damaged leg.

The war dragged on and on. On the home front we went about our daily routines. Many items were rationed: gasoline, sugar, tobacco, shoes, coffee–but somehow we survived. War Bonds which had tremendous growth potential, became a popular form of investment. Even at the elementary school level, special war stamps were sold to raise money for the war effort. Written communication with the military was done by air mail (called V-mail) in lightweight, sky blue envelopes which unfolded to become writing surfaces. Of course the military were restricted in the amount of information they could divulge about their location and activities.

Practically every family in town had a member serving in the armed forces. People who never before crossed paths would meet and commiserate over the way their loved ones were missed. There was an abundance of war movies, which were the main form of entertainment since television was yet to be available on a commercial basis. Since there were so many movie theaters in Albany, each developed ingenious ways to attract customers to their particular movie house. On Saturdays, dishes belonging to a set were given away in the hope that people would return and return–at least until they had accumulated a full set.

Usually a serial was also run with endings that enticed the customer to return to see the next episode. The *Tarzan* series was most popular with young teenaged boys. The movies were also a fine way to get the visual news which was invariably a part of the on screen offering.

Those were the days of the silver screen where stars like Bette Davis, Joan

Crawford, Olivia de Havilland, Joan Fontaine, Greer Garson, Rita Hayworth and Betty Grable drew the attention of the male population as Clark Gable, John Wayne, Tyrone Power, Alan Ladd, Jimmy Stewart, James Cagney and Walter Pigeon attracted the girls.

War-time music was devoted to swing, war songs and sentimental ballads. Some of the top performers were Glenn Miller, Bing Crosby, the Andrews Sisters, Dinah Shore, Lena Horne, Ella Fitzgerald, Kate Smith, Harry James, Guy Lombardo, the Dorsey Brothers and Duke Ellington.

We thought the war was sure to end in 1944, but a surprise resurgence of German military strength prolonged it another year. VE day was the decisive action by the Allies in Europe. After the invasion of the continent, Germany suffered reversal after reversal.

It took the atom bomb to bring the Japanese to surrender.

When the war was over, brothers Larry and Kim returned home. Brother Barry had recently joined the

Navy and in the future, brother Bleecker and I would follow in his footsteps.

November 22, 1963—The Assassination of President John F. Kennedy

There were an endless series of world disturbances following World War II. The Cold War with Russia went on for decades and became a part of our lives. Natural disasters, political and economic upheavals occurred over the years, but nothing could compare with the totally unexpected assassination of a US President on November 22, 1963.

John F. Kennedy was only in his third year of his first term in office and the era of *Camelot* pervaded the nation. He was an excellent orator, youthful and energetic. He hadn't enough time in office to accomplish much. We were admired by other nations because the Kennedy family image was so inspiring with its youth and vigor. Jackie was stylish, pretty and linguistically versatile. Their two young children, Caroline and Jack, Jr. were adorable.

And then tragedy struck. At a parade in Dallas, Texas, Lee Harvey Oswald shot and killed President Kennedy as he was being driven through the city in an open limousine.

The news was an unbelievable shock and just about everyone I know over 60 can clearly recall exactly what they were doing at the time the news came over the airwaves.

At that time, I was administering a test in the late afternoon at the Community College. The classroom door burst open and the Dean of Academic Affairs strode in and announced that the President had been fatally shot in Texas. The initial reaction of the students was total silence. I remember saying that the testing would continue, but I knew all was lost for that day. Several students simply walked out of the room in a state of shock. College classes were called off for the remainder of the day.

It was a strange sensation to walk the streets of our small city after the assassination. No one spoke. People just nodded with tears in their eyes. A cloud of disbelief hovered over everyone.

Then, of course, there were several days of TVs coverage of the traditional rites at the Rotunda, following the horse-drawn cortege and the funeral. The new president, Lyndon Johnson, had been sworn in aboard Air Force One and the transition went smoothly.

Not since the assassination of President William McKinley had the nation experienced such a similar shock—but in this era, the media provided immediate coverage.

September 11, 2001—The World Trade Center Attack

The terrorist attack which devastated the twin towers of the World Trade Center in Manhattan was the third occurrence in my lifetime which I felt to be truly mind altering. It was another of those rare events which becomes so indelibly fixed in memory that even the most minute details cannot be forgotten.

This was a first for the United States–an attack on the continental homeland by an outside force–and its effects have remained relatively undiminished. Sandy and I were preparing for a five-day visit with Pennsylvania friends to the horse country of Lexington, Kentucky. It was early in September, 2001, and I had a break from part time teaching. The weather for traveling was perfect–a crisp, clear autumn day.

We were just getting ready to start the car when the phone rang. It was my sister-in-law who was invariably the purveyor of bad news. Even the sound of her voice made me tense because I knew something negative was about to unfold.

"Have you been watching the TV?" she asked–and then immediately followed up by saying that a plane had deliberately smashed into one of the towers of the World Trade Center. "It's terrorists and they've come to kill us!" she warned.

"Kay," I calmly reasoned, "you are over-reacting. I'm sure it was a tragic accident." By this time Sandy had turned on the television and the news was out. It wasn't long after the first plane struck the north tower that a second plane targeted the south tower. Astonishingly, both towers quavered and then collapsed into a pile of dust and rubble but not before the cameras caught trapped individuals leaping to their death from the highest stories. The whole episode took only a few minutes, but it was mesmerizing to watch. Some 3,000 individuals lost their lives. Those who worked above the 85th floor had no chance at all. Below where the planes struck, however, police and fireman saved hundreds of lives.

The world was awestruck. An obscure Al-Qaida leader, Osama bin Laden from Saudi Arabia, had orchestrated the attack from Afghanistan. Months in advance, cells of terrorists had come into the USA with the expressed purpose of training to become suicide pilots. Their scheme worked perfectly. Attacks were orchestrated on the World Trade Center and the Pentagon with an additional attack foiled by passengers while their plane was on its way over western Pennsylvania to Washington DC.

Our friends from Pennsylvania phoned to say they would not be joining us on our trip to Kentucky, citing the danger that the world was currently in.

After driving about an hour and a half while listening to developments on the car radio, Sandy and I had second thoughts. Our son-in-law was an engineer on Amtrak railroads and would be taking a trip to New York City that day. With so much excitement going on there, my wife and I decided we should stay closer to home and I turned the car around.

We stayed overnight at home, keeping track of the aftermath of the attack. The next day we concluded that there wasn't really much to be accomplished by staying at home, and so once more drove off for a few days at Lexington, KY, horse country. Our five days in Kentucky were well spent. The fall weather was picture perfect and we sure learned a lot about horses. We visited the state capitol at Frankfurt and toured Ashland, the home of senator Henry Clay, a prominent political leader in the early part of the nineteenth century.

Other (for me) Memorable Happenings

The above three shocking events have been absorbed but not forgotten. There have been others less dynamic events which have contributed to memories— which just may have had an effect on my trauma upon reaching my 83rd birthday.

Recollecting past and present events leads me to the conclusion that those in my generation have probably witnessed more change than any other group. We started life at the beginning of the Great Depression. It wasn't until the 1940s that electricity came to the homestead. Shocking experiences such as the death of President Kennedy stunned the world. Other outstanding events during my era:

<u>The dropping of the atom bomb (1945)</u>: While this attack was so devastating to thousands of innocents, it has been calculated that thousands more would have died if conventional warfare had continued.

<u>The death of President Franklin D. Roosevelt (1945)</u>: After having been elected to a record fourth term in office and leading us through the Great Depression and World War II, President Roosevelt died at Warm Springs, GA. He'd been suffering from health issues for some time. For many he was a revered icon and his death came as a shock.

<u>The upset election of President Harry S. Truman (1948)</u>: Governor Thomas E. Dewey of New York State was considered a shoo-in by overwhelming expectations nationwide. Few expected "Give 'em Hell, Harry" to win but he did. A most prominent USA newspaper, the *Chicago Tribune* erroneously headlined that Dewey had won the election!

<u>The Interstate highway system (from coast to coast in the USA beginning in the 1940's)</u>. The first leg was the Pennsylvania Turnpike, followed by the Governor Thomas E. Dewey New York State Thruway in the 1950s and further extended by President Dwight

D. Eisenhower who wanted something similar to Germany's Autobahn which he had seen during WWII.

<u>The Cold War (the 50s through the 80s):</u> It wasn't long after the end of World War II that the Union of Socialist Soviet Republics (USSR) began to challenge the USA as a world power. Spheres of influence emerged. Nuclear warfare loomed as so much of a threat that here at home people were building underground shelters and school children were taught to crouch and cover under their desks in case of an attack.

Eventually, President Reagan negotiated with Prime Minister Gorbachev of the USSR at a time when the Soviet Union could no longer afford its defense costs, particularly with the threat of the USA to build an anti-ballistic missile shield. The Berlin Wall was torn down and the USSR dissolved into independent countries with Russia as the dominant nation.

<u>Space Exploration:</u> In the early 60s the Russians launched a manned rocket, *Sputnik*, into space. It stunned our nation that this could happen and soon we were in competition. Within a decade we had landed a man on the moon and launched ever so many exploratory spaceships and satellites.

<u>Civil Rights:</u> In the 1960's the civil rights movement gained momentum with the racial clashes in Selma,

Alabama. Dr. Martin Luther King became the prominent spokesman for African Americans and, after so many demonstrations and confrontations, Civil Rights legislation was enacted by Congress under the leadership of President Lyndon B. Johnson.

<u>Women's Movement:</u> The right of women to gain equality with men in the workplace was a spirited movement spearheaded by Gloria Steinem, Bella Abzug, and other prominent spokeswomen. The Equal Rights Amendment to the Constitution was proposed but never ratified by enough states. However, the enactment of Title IX which required schools to divide their athletic budgets between male and females was a landmark victory for female athletes.

<u>Rock and Roll:</u> It is my observation that most people's favorite music is what was popular when they were in their teens and early 20s. For me that meant the big band and swing era and the gentle love songs of the '50s. That all changed dramatically when hip-gyrating Elvis Presley took over the music world followed by the Beatles and the Rolling Stones. Rap and hip-hop have since become the rage.

<u>The Rise of China:</u> When World War II ended, the USA lost a military ally, Nationalist China, headed by General Chiang-Kai-Shek. The cultural revolution of the '60s resulted in rule by a communist government, chaired by Mao Tse-tung. Under successive administrations, China, with the largest population in the world,

has become second only to the United States as a world power.

The Vietnam War: We should have learned a very important lesson in this several-year tragedy which costs thousands and thousands of lives unnecessarily. The odds of winning in terms of numbers and location were insurmountable and somehow we should have relied more upon negotiations than military involvement.

President Richard M. Nixon Resigns: Disgraced by proof that he was involved in the Watergate break-in of the Democratic headquarters, Nixon resigned rather than face impeachment. It was sad and unnecessary because the Republicans already had the election sewed up.

Technology advances: Throughout the latter half of the 20th century and up to current times, the advances in technology have been unprecedented. Not only in the computer area, but also in the building trade, medicine, automotive and communications. The Internet and Wi-fi have revolutionized access to information causing dramatic changes in such areas as shopping, communication and data management. Social media has become a phenomena affecting all walks of national and international life, including war. Cell phones, smart phones, and IPads all proliferated to the extent that they have become so universally accepted and relied upon that recollection of the pre-technology era is almost lost.

The Reagan Presidency (1980-88): Philosophically, I'm a conservative Republican who, among other things, favor less government intervention in our lives– but at the same time endorse global markets and setting a path toward full citizenship for illegal immigrants. Reagan's compromising abilities, affable nature, and devotion to his wife are much to be admired.

President Bill Clinton's Indiscretion: President Clinton was impeached for lying to a congressional committee about his sexual involvement with an aide, Monica Lewinsky. He was not convicted, however.

The Lesbian/Gay/Bisexual/Transgender movement (LGBT): Minority recognition has been a hallmark of the 20th and 21st centuries with the result that, at last, much prejudice has subsided and acceptance is gradually emerging.

Recessions: In the early 2000s came the recession when the economy faltered over serious problems in the financial world. In 2008 there was another recession involving problems in the housing market.

Mid-East conflicts: In the latter part of the 20th Century and up until current times, the USA has been involved in a series of wars in the Middle East. First came the Gulf War in the 1990s, followed by the Iraq and Afghanistan wars in the 2000s, and on to the Syrian conflict. The latest involvement involves ISIS and our attempt to rid the world of this terrorist group that often operates world wide.

The Arab Spring: It began in Egypt and the overthrow of the Mubarak dictatorship. Coups successfully took over the governments of Tunisia, Libya and Yemen with support coming from neighboring states and the world powers.

The 2016 presidential race: Not since the Chicago riots at the Democratic Convention of 1964 do I recall such contention during a presidential election year. Donald Trump has stimulated some provocative dialogue and even suggested possible physical violence which could have disastrous after effects.

Three

FAMILY BACKGROUND

The early ancestors

The Staats family in America dates back to colonial times when the Dutch settled what is now eastern New York State. They did this through the patroon system, whereby wealthy merchants in the Netherlands colonized early New York State by sending settlers over to work the land and to trap beavers, paying rent to the Patroon in return for the privilege of having some acreage of their own in the new world. The Patroon who sponsored the first of my family to immigrate was Killian Van Rensselaer, who never set foot in New Netherlands, the Dutch name for what later became New York State. The colonization took place under the direction of the Dutch West India Company.

The earliest ancestor was Abram Staats who was born in the Netherlands in 1617 and came to the colonies in 1642. He was a surgeon. As I understand it, surgeons in those days started out as barbers–which has everything to do with barber poles having red (blood) and white (bandages) stripes. Abram broadened his horizons by becoming a fur trader. Back then, beaver pelts were used to make expensive items of apparel in Europe, particularly fur hats in Russia.

In addition, Abram became a pilot on sloops plying the Hudson River, and in later life, he became a magistrate in the city of Albany, New York, which was originally called Fort Orange. Our earliest ancestor died at the age of 73, a respected old age at the time.

Abram had several children–among them Joachim who in 1696 completed building a fieldstone house, Hoogebergh, on a knoll on the east bank of the Hudson some five miles below Albany. This homestead has been owned and occupied by the Staats family for twelve generations to date.

The first several generations were farmers who tirelessly worked the land and who probably had little time or energy for keeping records. Hence, little is known of their lives. One particular ancestor deserves mention.

In the family cemetery at the top of the hill overlooking the homestead is a gravestone honoring Col. Philip Staats, who was injured in the Revolutionary War as he served with General George Washington in the Continental Army. Other than the colonel, few family ancestors were prominently known.

The Seventh Generation—grandparents

With such limited information regarding the earlier generations, let us move on to those in more recent times. Recollections of my grandparents (the seventh generation) come only from conversations overheard from older members of my family, since both sets of grandparents died before I reach the age of one. My mother's maiden name was Smith, and she was born in 1895 in Rensselaer, a small city across the Hudson River from Albany, New York.

There is a sepia-toned photo of grandmother Smith (nee Agnes Stitt) on the wall at the homestead. She looks prim and proper, dressed in a high-necked white blouse with her hair in ringlets piled high on her head. No pole dancer, that one!

Grandfather Smith of Scot/Northern Ireland descent, must have been a real bundle of joy to live with. He was very active in the Salvation Army. In my mom's early years, Sundays consisted of several hours of church followed by limited activity for the rest of the day. Movie attendance was forbidden, as were cards and other parlor games. Even reading comic strips in the newspapers was not allowed!

I'm told that Grandfather Smith died suddenly while babysitting. My older brothers found him in the hallway lying flat on this back with his feet up in the air off the floor. Apparently, he'd suffered a fatal heart attack. At the time, Brother Garrett was in his high chair waiting to be fed. Brother Barry told everyone, "Grandpa was lying down."

Grandfather Lawrence Anthony Staats is more interesting. He was a partner in a firm that ran a huge ice house on the homestead property. It was one of several ice houses along the Hudson. It was a few hundred feet from the river and it was immense. It was so large that it blocked the view down the river from the house. Records indicate that the wooden ice house held some 10,000 tons of ice and was about 100 feet wide, 150 feet long, and six stories high. The ice was cut from the river and hauled by horse-drawn sled to a conveyor ramp which carried it into the huge structure for storage. There the ice was covered with a protective layer of sawdust to keep it from melting. In the warmer months barges pulled in at Staats Landing, were loaded with ice, and traveled as far south as New York City and even points east as far as Boston.

In addition to the ice house, Grandfather Staats was also involved in managing a feed store in the city of Rensselaer in partnership with his two brothers,

Wil and Phil. Lawrence (Larry)'s role in these joint ventures was to act as an agent, often occupying an apartment in New York City. He traveled between the homestead and the big city.

Somewhere along the way, he met and married Jennie Ostrum, a young lady who loved the bright lights and excitement of the big city and hated the desolation and quietness at the homestead. She dabbled in painting and left behind as a remembrance, a replica oil painting of the family crest of arms which–according to family folklore–had been granted to the family by the Estates General (government) of the Netherlands for an ancestor's valor in helping to defeat the Spanish Armada in 1588 when it attacked England and the Netherlands.

Lawrence Anthony Staats, although very prominent in business, is buried in an unmarked grave in the family cemetery which, incidentally, he willed to the Dutch Reformed Church in East Greenbush. Why is this important? If the family instead of the church owned the cemetery, there would be an annual cemetery fee and limitations imposed by the State in terms of health regulations. Since the church owns it, we continue to be able to use the cemetery for internments.

The Eighth Generation--Parents' Siblings

The Smith grandparents had five children. The eldest was my uncle Merrill. I recall from my early youth that he was in poor health and, consequently, mean spirited. I understand that in younger years he traveled as a blacksmith with Ringling Brothers and Barnum & Bailey Circus. He would tell stories about Moduk, a huge elephant featured in circus advertising. I have no reason to doubt the rumors that Uncle Merrill died from syphilis, since that seemed to produce his surly disposition and ultimately caused his demise in his 50s.

William Smith (Uncle Will) was the second born of the Smith offspring. Since they lived in limited financial circumstances, he left school in the third grade to work as a milk delivery boy and later in life went to work on the New York Central Railroad. He may not have had much schooling, but he was one of the wisest and finest men I have ever known. In his adult years, he was promoted to be an engineer of the New York Central coal-fired behemoths plying the rails between Albany and New York City. The job paid well during the Great Depression years.

For my mother and my siblings, Uncle Will was truly a savior. My father died accidentally in his early 50s leaving behind my mom with seven young children. There was no insurance, pension or hospitalization at the time, and the family would have had go to foster homes or to try to exist on the *county dole* (welfare) a mere pittance back in the early 1930s.

Uncle Will stepped into the breach. This bachelor uncle and his maiden sister, Bess, opened the doors of their rented row house to our family–no questions asked. He felt the obligation and carried the burden without complaint. For approximately twenty years we were fed and housed by this generous uncle. He loved children and was particularly thoughtful on special occasions. I recall looking forward to the 4th of July holidays when he would arrive at the homestead with boxes and boxes of fireworks.

In return for sharing Uncle Will's home, we growing children helped with the household chores which included carrying out coal ashes and toting pails of drinking water from a neighbor's well. We had to keep quiet when Uncle Will was sleeping. He worked a variety of shifts on the railroad and often slept during the day, a tough time for five growing boys to be quiet. He relied on the telephone for receiving calls to go to work, so occupying the phone was another family no-no. As we matured, we were expected to attend school regularly and to do homework. In our teen years, we helped out with carpentry, painting, wallpapering and vehicle repair projects.

In 1937 my mom acquired a used 1931 Model A Ford Roadster from the hired hand next door, who had to choose between drinking and driving as directed by the local sheriff. The car enabled my family to provide some relief for our uncle and aunt when we drove away to the homestead on weekends and stayed there in the summer.

Uncle Will suffered miserably from asthma for most of his adult life. In order to breathe properly, he slept semi-upright in a Morse chair which had an adjustable back rest. Eventually the toll of asthma affected his heart, and he died of congestive heart failure at the age of 67.

Aunt Bess was the third of my grandparents' five children, and she was truly another saint, albeit a strict one. She never married. When Mom became widowed and our huge family moved in, Aunt Bess left her job as a clerk in a large Albany department store and occupied herself as housekeeper for the family while Mom cleaned houses and did some caregiving in the local area.

My aunt Bess led an active social life. She played bridge with the neighbor ladies and participated in our church dart league. She even played a leading role in a church group's production of *Snow White*. I can clearly recall her coughing up a chunk of the poisoned apple after the prince arrived and kissed her as she lay in the coffin. The apple bit must have flown ten feet!

She would dramatically re-enact her bridge games to my mother in the late evening after returning from a match. "Sarah was a sly fox as she held onto that trump," she once waxed enthusiastically. At another time, the ladies had given the birthday gift of a roll of toilet paper to a regular attendant of the bridge set together with the notation that "a friend in need is a friend indeed." Apparently, the *birthday girl* wasn't at all pleased.

Aunt Bess would sit for hours and hours playing games with us when we were very young. *Parcheesi*, a board game exotically billed as *The Royal Game of India*, was a favorite. Later in life, I met someone who spent several years in India and had never heard of the game while there. Our favorite card games were *Casino* and *Pelmanism* (sometimes called *Concentration*).

There was also a game called *Pick-Up Sticks*. The object of that game was to delicately remove one stick from a scattered pile without disturbing any of the others. As a last resort, a player who was sure he couldn't accomplish that goal could smash his fist down on the pile and thus rearrange the sticks. Apparently Aunt Bess did not like that option, and brother Bleecker would exercise it repeatedly in spite of her disapproval. One day she must have been in a bad mood, because the third time Bleecker used the *smashing* option, she stood up and scattered the sticks by hand onto the floor of the room and then proceeded to storm out of the room, slamming the door behind her. Bleeck and I knew enough to lay low until the storm had settled.

And then there was Gekko!

Aunt Bess had a fertile imagination involving a pet toy grey monkey, a foot-long stuffed miniature of the real thing. *Gekky* would appear rarely, with Aunt Bess playing the ventriloquist. The monkey would talk to us animatedly about his personal life, his activities, his preferred food (bananas, of course) and how he would spend his winters in Florida enjoying the warm weather which tropical animals preferred. Bleeck and I loved the repertoire and our aunt's vivid imagination. To add mystery to the pretension, Aunt Bess would hide Gekko in her bureau drawer for the winter months. We would beg her to let Gekko *come home* from Florida so that we could spend more time with him. Aunt Bess would demur with the excuse that Gekky loved Florida too much to come back during cold weather.

Bleeck, in his inimitable fashion, somehow unexpectedly came across the monkey hidden cleverly under lingerie in the bureau drawer. Of course, he had no right to be rummaging in the drawer, but that was his nature. He rushed up to Aunt Bessie with Gekko in hand. "Aunt Bessie, I found Gekko. He doesn't go to Florida after all!"

Aunt Bessie's response? A resounding swat on the butt that just about sent Bleeck sprawling.

In addition to being a fun game partner, Aunt Bess was an excellent cook. Some things that are now pricey must have been relatively cheap during the Great Depression, because I remember frequent meals of leg of lamb or oyster stew, which are somewhat dear in present times. We always had well balanced meals with plenty of vegetables and fruit which Bleeck, of course, disdained. If he could get away with it, he would focus only on mashed potatoes, meat and gravy. Aunt Bess nicknamed him *potato water* because of his preferences.

Her humor extended to meal times. Toward the end of the main course, she would often ask, "And who would like some chocolate cream pie?" All of us would respond enthusiastically. But that is as far as it went. There was no chocolate pie and Aunt Bess just wanted to test our gullibility.

Sometimes Aunt Bess didn't abide by her favorite creed, "Don't let your wit run away with you," which was the subject of her frequent lectures to the growing youngsters. We had a sixth grade teacher named Mae O'Grady and she was as Irish as Paddy's pig. To her, the north of Ireland with its Protestantism and orange symbolism was an anathema. Knowing this, Aunt Bess would dress us in orange sweatshirts and send us off to school on St. Patrick's Day. What an obvious insult to the wearing of the green extolled by Miss O'Grady. And how did she react? With an angry shudder she sent us home to change into something less inflammatory!

On Friday evenings during the school year, my mother would pack us all into the Model A Ford and drive off to the homestead in order to give her bachelor brother and maiden sister some rest. Here again, Aunt Bess would exercise her great sense of humor. She would stand on the front stoop and loudly sing out *Happy Days Are Here Again* which happened to be Franklin D. Roosevelt's campaign song. We were staunch Republicans, but the song seemed appropriate for the occasion.

Time took its toll on this dear caretaker. In her early 60s, Aunt Bess succumbed to dementia. Uncharacteristically she would smear her face with rouge and apply heavy doses of lipstick. She would sit on the front porch smoking cigarettes, something else she never did in earlier days. Eventually, her heart gave out and she, too, died of congestive heart failure at the age of 63.

The fourth oldest of the Smith offspring was Uncle Allen. He served the army in the trenches in World War I and, I recall, brought home his doughboy uniform which included a gas mask. He did not marry until his 50s and in his younger years spent a great deal of time at the homestead with our family. Uncle Allen was always easy going and in good humor. He loved children and thoroughly enjoyed our antics as youngsters.

Uncle Allen worked as a conductor on the railroad. Sometimes he slept at the railroad YMCA near the train stations in New York City and in Albany. He was always on hand to pitch in with work projects at the homestead.

In later years he married Aunt Gail who was, by far, the dominant role in the twosome. She was striking in appearance using just the right amount of makeup and jet black hair coloring.

Her background was Italian, Catholic and–lord forbid–she had been divorced. She and my mother did not hit it off initially because of my mother's WASP views, but, once we all got to know and appreciate her, we had frequent social get-togethers playing cards or just visiting.

Oh, could that woman exaggerate! "I knocked that son-of-a-bitch all the way down the stairs," she related, regarding a dispute with her son-in-law. Or, "Esther, I had to crawl on my hands and knees three blocks through the snow I felt so weak." There had to be a vague element of truth in there somewhere.

After a time, Uncle Allen's health failed and he, too died of congestive heart failure–at the age of 72. Aunt Gail lived on for several years, and eventually died at the age of 85 after what she proclaimed were literally dozens of heart attacks.

The youngest of the Smith offspring, Esther (my mother), is described in the next segment.

My father had only one sibling, about whom I know very little. Apparently Aunt Mabel and my father were estranged and I suspect it had something to do with the breakup of her marriage. Apparently, while enjoying a winter honeymoon at Niagara Falls, Aunt Mabel and her husband were overlooking the falls when she removed her hand from her fur muff and out slipped a note. Her husband picked up the note and read it. The note to Aunt Mabel was from a gentleman friend with whom she's had a long term relationship. The marriage ended abruptly.

The only other information I know of Aunt Mabel is that she died destitute in a county home in Newburgh. When my brothers Larry and Kim got out of the service following World War II, they searched for her. She had passed away only a few weeks earlier as a ward of the city of Newburgh, dying intestate, and the boys settled with the city.

The Eighth Generation (Cont'd)--Parents

When I was only nine months old, my father, Lawrence A. Staats (called Arthur) died at age 51. On a late autumn day in 1932, he slipped and fell near the homestead and broke his leg.

A blood clot ensued which ended his life. In those days, it was customary to have the viewing at home. I'm also told that we were experiencing flooding of some three feet of water over the dirt road leading through the lowland fields and that the casket on a wagon was drawn by wading horses.

I know little of my dad. I know he remained a bachelor until age 37 and then married and had seven children, one girl followed by six boys. In his youth he was quite an outdoorsman, particularly fond of hunting and boating. He was heavy set and barrel chested. He was very strict and had a temper. He took no nonsense from his children, responding swiftly to bad language and mischief.

He was most annoyed by my mother's handwriting which was notoriously undecipherable. Often he would come home furious after being unable to read her hand-written grocery list. He couldn't stand clutter. In one instance he banged his head against a metal cooking pot hanging in the cellar. With that he opened the cellar door and the kitchen door leading to the outside. Once the doors were opened, he threw every hanging pot and pan out onto the front yard–as my mother stood by in tears.

Despite his occasional bouts with bad temper, my father had a fine sense of humor as evidenced by a series of photos he had made of himself making hilarious faces way back in the 1920s. My brothers also recall him looking out toward the driveway during mealtime and occasionally jumping up from his chair and exclaiming, "Well, here they are!" Since we lived in the country, visitors were a very exciting change of pace and we would all abandon the table and run toward the parking lot to greet the company. Only there was no company–it was just a trick daddy played on us and it worked every time.

During Prohibition in the early 1920s, there was a club house facing the river on the knoll above the house. Apparently attached to the club house was a small building which contained a still for brewing alcohol, a federal offense at the time. One day, a truck full of federal agents sped into the homestead parking lot. Out jumped several G-Men and stormed up the hill, axes in hand. They smashed the still and all related nearby materials used in the processing.

Following that incident, my father, who was living at the homestead at the time, was questioned by the law enforcement group. He pleaded not guilty to knowing anything about the operation, even though it was a short distance from the homestead. Dad pointed out that there existed another access road to the still which ran through the next door property and that he knew nothing about the illegal goings on. Because it could not be proved that he was familiar with the operation, he was let off the hook.

Daddy worked as a clerk in the feed store co-owned by his father and two uncles. His wages were meager and, at the time of his death, he had little to leave behind.

There are not enough words of praise to describe my mother, Esther Finlay Staats.

She was one in a million—admired by all who knew her. With her strict, Scot-Irish upbringing, she took life's setbacks in stride without complaint. She had studied to become a teacher at the two-year teaching normal school which later became the State Teachers' College of Albany—and is now the University at Albany.

She taught for a year or two and she hated it. Restless fifth graders were not her cup of tea.

At one time my father was courting Aunt Bess. This lasted some time until my dad shifted his affections to my mother, Bess's younger sister. When they married, he was 37 and she was in her early 20s. While courting, they would take long walks at the homestead. On one occasion, Armistice Day (now Veterans Day) in 1918, he dared her to take his 22 caliber rifle and shoot a bottle off the top of his head. She proceeded to do just that. That cemented the relationship. Their decision to marry was sudden. One afternoon at around 4 p.m. mother phoned her best friend, Bertelle Wornham, and ask what Bertelle's plans were for the evening. "I have nothing scheduled. Why do you ask?" Bertelle inquired. Mother's response: "Arthur and I are being married this evening and would like you to serve as Maid of Honor!" That was that.

Fourteen years and seven children later, my father died unexpectedly.

Esther was widowed with six young children and very little in terms of financial resources. I was only a 9-month old baby. A month before my father died, brother Gary set his bed afire while playing with matches. After some time in the hospital, he returned home and was convalescing when he contracted a strep germ that proved to be fatal. This was in November. Mother had no transportation or telephone, a rare commodity in those days. Dad was at work some five miles away in Rensselaer. Incredibly, mother rowed our boat across the river where she knew a neighbor who had a phone. She called for help but Gary never recovered. I cannot help but wonder how this woman survived the death of one child, followed by the birth of another, followed by the death of her husband–all within the span of several months.

Mother had to contend with even more than the loss of two loved ones and the birth of a new baby. In addition to meager financial resources, she lived in a homestead that had no electricity or indoor plumbing, with the exception of a spigot that allowed for drawing cold water from an outdoor rain container tank. Heat was provided by wood stoves. After the fires were lit using kindling wood and newspaper, they required constant attention. And of course, the kindling wood had to be splintered by axe from larger blocks of wood.

Where did the blocks come from? At the homestead, gathering and cutting up wood was an annual chore, usually done at Thanksgiving time. My uncles and my teen aged brothers and a few friends would do the work. Used railroad ties, an undesirable wood because of its heavy pitch content (which caused soot that could lead to chimney fires) were carried by truck or Model A Ford to the homestead. There the ties, weighing over 80 pounds, were fed into a buzz saw where a huge, menacing blade cut the wood into stove-sized blocks. The whole operation took a few days and provided enough wood for a year. Of course, the cut up wood had to be stacked under shelter. It was the younger boys' chore to chop the wood into kindling and to carry the wood as well as the kindling into the house. At one time, we had three or four stoves going just to keep the drafty homestead comfortable.

Although we had a tap faucet running rainwater into the kitchen, the drinking water well was 200 feet away from the house. The potable water had to be carried by hand, and Mother and the older brothers shouldered that unending task for at least ten years until brother Kim had a trench dug and installed a pipeline between the kitchen and the well.

In the kitchen there was a pail of well water near the sink which had a dipper and, although not the height of sanitation, anyone needing a drink used the dipper.

We never did install an indoor john or central heating system. To this day, the privy consists of two small outhouses: one standard *three-holer* for the guys and a much newer compost toilet for the ladies and guests.

In the 1930s life for housewives was so much more physically challenging than today in so many ways. I recall watching my mother iron clothes. To begin with, she hated housework and was much happier flower gardening, painting, visiting with friends, swimming and just puttering out of door at a variety of tasks. Ironing was a real chore. Once the wood stove was fired up, she would place three or four heavy cast iron hand irons on the stove, flat side down. When they were hot, she would select an iron and begin pressing clothing, sheets, etc. Often she would be neglectful and leave the iron to linger, causing a brown burned stain on the garment. Once the iron cooled down, she would grab another one, protecting her hands by using a cloth potholder. No wonder she hated the job.

Washing clothes was another of my mother's onerous tasks. We had a gas-operated washing machine complete with a ringer–a truly threatening device. When feeding clothes through the ringer, one had to be careful not to let one's fingers get fed into the rollers. The damned gas-operated motor was temperamental and the fumes from the engine were suffocating. For the truly obstinate stains, a scrub board was required involving even more manual work.

We had a cow, Georgiana. While a gentle beast, she could be stubborn, particularly when it came to getting her into the barn for milking. In wintertime the cow required hay and feed, which came from my uncles' feed store. Needless to say, we had fresh milk all year round, but in the early spring when the cow ate wild onions, the milk was repulsive to swallow. But swallow it we did, because of Mother's unyielding *guidance*. Georgiana was particularly difficult when she was calving. Just before she was about to give birth, she would disappear into a nearby swampy area and hide among the trees. My mother would get so frustrated trying to herd the damned cow that she burst into tears and resort to language which she never would use otherwise. I remember the cow having two or three offspring and pulling the same stunt each time.

Mother took her commitment to enforcing our behavior seriously. Sister Jane was always a model of behavior, but the six boys were a challenge. When dad was alive, he would be greeted daily by Jane when he got home from work. Although she never wrote it down, she would clearly detail every misdeed her brothers engaged in and relate them to her father, whereupon he would mete out punishment, which usually took the form of a swat or two on the behind. This pleased sister Jane immensely.

After daddy passed on, Mother embraced her responsibility for discipline in a no-nonsense fashion. We were not allowed to use off-color language, including such harmless words as *stink* or *damned*. Her punishment was usually a severe tongue lashing or, when truly perturbed, a lilac switch. The older brothers loved to see punishment administered to us younger ones and brother Kim, in particular, would cheerfully cut off a lilac switch for mother's use.

Not long after the loss of our father, Uncle Will and Aunt Bess opened their house in Rensselaer to our sizeable family. This was done to provide security for our family and to prevent sending us to foster care. It had the benefit of providing access to the Rensselaer public school system. My mother earned some money by cleaning and caregiving in nearby homes, but she also maintained tight control over her brood. Aunt Bess did the housework and cooking and children entertaining, and Uncle Will brought home the bacon. That was our arrangement throughout our childhood—and it worked extremely well.

On weekends we would go to the homestead and we would also stay there once school was out for the summer. In the fall it was back to school and to city living. In a way, we had a balanced living style, urban as well as rural.

Mother aged and became more mellow as the years passed. She was proud of her family and was able to relax somewhat. World War II came as a blow because she immediately lost her eldest two sons to the Navy. Later on, Brothers Barry and Bleeck and I also went to that branch of the service even though it wasn't wartime.

The war years were tough, exacerbated by the rationing of shoes, sugar, coffee, gasoline and other items. Because of her hardship status, mother was granted a *B* classification for purchase of gas thanks to city authorities who recognized her need to drive the Model A back and forth to the homestead.

Brothers Larry and Kim were sorely missed but it made us only more aware of the war. Kim saw duty aboard a submarine in the Pacific and Larry spent time on a PT Boat patrolling in the Philippines. Neither of them was injured although Kim qualified for partial hearing disability caused by the loud diesel engines of the submarine.

On the home front, we all did our patriotic duties, among other things adhering to strict enforcement of blackout rules when houses were darkened at night in response to mock air raids. Once in a while we bent the rules by neglecting to turn out the lights, thereby bringing a volunteer warden knocking at the door.

Uncle Will loved to chew tobacco, a filthy but ingrained habit. His brand was Havana Blossom Plain which came in a strawberry colored package. The Rudnick's store in Albany consistently stocked it. We all loved going to Rudnick's because it had the fascinating smell of leather boots, and it also had a unique vacuum system for transmitting transactions between the downstairs customers and the upstairs office. I suppose we were abusing the rationing system by having us nephews go into the store separately with each of us purchasing the allocated single package of tobacco. In those war years, there was no age restriction for buying tobacco.

Another World War ll memory involved proudly hanging of a window flag with a blue star or stars to represent the number of family members away in the armed services. I think at one time that our home flag had three stars.

The patriotism was contagious and we never missed the evening radio news broadcast. No one had a TV until after the war. The names of those Pacific Islands being recaptured from the Japanese were intriguing- -Saipan, Tarawa, Bougainvillea, Guam, Wake Island. We relearned world geography daily.

Among the adults there was constant communication about family members in the service. Tears of joy and tears of sorrow were shared lovingly.

Patriotism in the entertainment world was ubiquitous, thanks to organizations like the USO. The Andrews Sisters and Bing Crosby were at the top of the hits list, selling millions of 78 speed records churning out wildly popular songs like *Hot Time in the Town of Berlin.* and *Don't Fence Me In.* War bonds were sold to help finance the war. Kate Smith sang *God Bless America* and was a top-notch bond seller and entertainer.

Mother weathered the temporary loss of her children. We were all busy sending Air Mail letters and awaiting a response. Mother's penmanship was an item of amused concern for those away from home. M's ran into N's and W's in what appeared to be an endless succession of small waves. Letters I and T respectively were dotted and crossed at the end of a line. Afterthoughts were often scrawled around the margin of the paper so that one would *pinwheel* the paper while reading the letter. The fun thing is that we'd all grown to an age where we would be critical without being reprimanded.

School behavior was constantly monitored by both the teachers and the principal. Getting out of line wasn't an option. It seemed the teaching staff during the entire school years became a part of our extended family. Deviation in school behavior was immediately given home notification and we were subject to correction both at the school and at home.

Practical and *resourceful* are two adjectives which seem to best describe my mother. When a problem arose she dealt with it without hesitation and in accordance with her instinctive convictions. On the highway she was a menace. I don't think there was one fender on the Model A which hadn't been repaired or replaced. The poor car was often overburdened, sometimes with as many as 10 or 11 passengers. We were young and we thoroughly enjoyed riding on the fenders or standing on the running board or the luggage rack and cramming into the rumble seat as well as the creature comfort of riding in the passenger seat. Obviously, traffic laws were much more relaxed in those days. Besides, most of the police knew and respected my mother in spite of her dubious driving skills.

For deviltry, we cooked up a stunt that would upset Mother—but which she could not control. There is a wide highway bridge on Rte. 9&20 which we would pass under when returning on Rte. 9J from the homestead to Rensselaer. It was wide and had an echo. With Mother concentrating on her driving, we would mischievously in union shout out *cat shit* and enjoy the echo. Mother wasn't pleased. She would shout out admonitions but they weren't enough to stifle our giggling.

I recall her once attempting to pass a car on our two lane highway. The Model A could only accelerate to 45 mph or so. When she got even with the car she was attempting to pass, another one came barreling toward us from the opposite direction. Mother had one of four choices: (a) become involved in a head on crash, (b) veer off the highway and into a ditch on the left (c) drop back behind the car she was passing, or (d) cut off the car she was passing. The decision had to be made instantly and she opted for (d). In the process of cutting the guy off, she managed to mangle his left front fender. Both cars came to a screeching halt. The driver of the damaged car was livid and he lit into Mother with a volley of oath-filled accusations. Her response? She fired back in kind, intimidating the guy by saying:

"Why didn't you slow down and let me pass, you goddamned fool?" He was completely unnerved by her vigorous challenge.

"But look what you've done to my fender," he continued

"That little dent?" mother said, minimizing the crumpled metal. "My boys can fix that in no time at all," she continued. I don't recall how the incident was settled but I know the man returned to his car defeated.

There was another time when her resourcefulness came into play. Mother had invited an old friend to the homestead for the day and we were returning to the city in the Model A taking a seldom used route on the way home. It was winter and it was getting dark. I was in the middle of the front seat and our guest was sitting on the right. Suddenly a battery terminal under the floorboard began to spark and then the wood flooring burst into a small fire. Anyone else would have been frightened silly. Not Mother. She instantly opened a half emptied bottle of milk we had with us and doused the potential fire. Following that, we all got back into the car and went on our way.

If the country roads were a challenge, just imagine her driving along crowded city streets! There she was truly a tiger. I was a passenger with her one time driving down South Pearl Street in Albany. It was approaching 5 p.m. and the traffic was heavy. Mother had perfected cutting people off, and she did so a couple of times with the audible result of brakes screeching and curse words being exchanged.

At one intersection, having nearly been run over by the Model A, a pedestrian called out, "Hey Grandma, if you can't drive it then park the damned car!" Had Mother known the meaning of the middle finger gesture she may have used it, although foul hand signals were not a part of her persona.

She loved ice cream. Once I heard her lament that ice cream didn't come in large round containers to enable anyone to get their head inside and lick out the remaining contents.

Her cooking was not that great–except for pies, apple fritters and doughnuts. At those she excelled. She hated cooking almost as much as she hated housework. When at the homestead, Mother took over the cooking chore. Burnt toast and oatmeal were the standard fare for breakfast. It almost seemed cruel to me that we were forced to eat a burned breakfast on Christmas mornings before we were allowed to tackle opening the presents.

When I joined the Navy and ate meals with guys from all around the USA, I would often hear grumbling about the meals dished out. "This isn't like my mother's cooking," my companions would often lament. To which I would respond, "Thank God for that!"

She loved to swim and therefore our growing brood were constantly swimming in the Hudson River in warmer weather. It isn't surprising that my son made a career as a SEAL in the Navy. In the water, Mom would follow the easy pace of the breast stroke. In her 60's, she continued her love for swimming and often organized a large group to swim the quarter-of-a-mile span of the Hudson and back again.

When she reached 65, we called a halt to her marathon swimming, based solely on the fear that if something went wrong, friends would wonder why we let Mother take such a chance at her age. In later years, my attitude toward swimming the river changed. After all, swimming is not tiring unless you are out of shape or are racing. A leisurely-paced breast stroke can be maintained for hours at a time, even when one is far into the golden years.

As the years passed and our family matured, we came to truly appreciate what a special person we had as a mother and we treated her accordingly. She loved being a passenger on long rides and was particularly fond of driving out to Buffalo, some three hundred miles west, to visit sister Jane where her husband took a job and their family stayed for several years.

She was always included in family gatherings and we gradually got to the point where we could kid with her in a friendly way. When she lost her teeth, she would lisp while using some words. One time a nest of honey-bees had settled in the walls of the rock garden. "What is it mom?" we inquired. Her response: "Beeves." And she said "geeves" instead of geese. She sure heard that repeated enough times in a teasing way. We kidded her about mispronouncing such places as "Bimmington (Binghamton), Mazzachusheets (Massachusetts), and Coliphoneia (California)."

Mother hated air travel. She was deathly afraid of riding in an airplane. One time, when I was first married, my wife and I persuaded her to take a seaplane ride with us at Long Lake, NY, at the height of the fall foliage season. The foliage was amazingly colorful and we knew it would be even more spectacular looking down from the sky. Mother reluctantly agreed to come along. I sat up front with the pilot and she and my wife were in the back. Mother was obviously shaken by the entire adventure. When we got far above the Adirondacks, the pilot tipped the plane up on its side so that Mother could fully enjoy the view looking straight down several hundred feet. I looked back to see if she was enjoying herself. Instead of enjoying it she was terrified and held her eyes tightly shut. She heaved a sigh of relief when we deplaned. Sandy and I, on the other hand, had thoroughly enjoyed the experience.

Brother Larry once decided to move to the Seattle area. He would take a job in some engineering capacity for a few years, and if things worked out, he planned to remain there. Before he decided to return home a few years later, he asked Mother to fly out to the state of Washington to enjoy an extended drive down the west coast as far as Los Angeles. Although she dearly wanted to enjoy the drive, she was adamant against the flight. A family council was held. We shared the expense of a ticket and brow beat Mother into bearing with the discomfort of the flight. She took the plane. But she hated the experience. When Larry met her at the Seattle airport, she was badly shaken and wasn't able to be her natural self for a day or two.

However, she thoroughly enjoyed the driving segment of the trip, and delighted in making phone calls
home along the way, breezily raving about her experiences in *San* (San Francisco) and *Los* (Los Angeles).
Once home, she never stopped talking about it.

After Uncle Will died, we converted the house into
upstairs and downstairs apartments with Mother occupying the bottom floor and Sandy and I and the children
at the top. A few years later when our family, including
a Great Dane dog, increased we needed more room
and moved and became tenants in the north wing of
the homestead which we rented from my brother Kim.
In the meantime, Mother took in tenants.

Near the end of our stay in the upstairs apartment,
my mother had a cat named Reeves. The large male
tabby developed a most interesting habit. When he felt
the need to relieve himself by urinating he would jump
into the empty bathtub and squat over the drain. In all
other situations he would use the cat box. Not only was
this interesting to me, but I thought it to be very clever
and within the boundaries of sanitation.

As a matter of fact, we were all proud of Reeves.
Until one day.

Toward the end of our stay, Mother started showing the second floor apartment to prospective tenants.
On one occasion, she was chatting with a prospect before mounting the stairs to show him the flat. As they

climbed the stairs, Reeves raced up the stairs, darted between their legs and bee-lined it for the bathtub.

In distress, Mother shouted, "STOP THE CAT!"

Too late. Reeves competed his mission–and we lost the prospective tenant.

Toward the end of her sixties Mom began to fail. Instead of working in the flower garden she would sit on the veranda for hours, enjoying the view. It just wasn't like her to rest for such long periods. She had mellowed to the extent that she would enjoy an occasional glass of wine, a taboo for her in earlier years. Eventually she began to suffer from mini strokes which left her partially paralyzed. She was practically incapacitated when she suffered attacks of vertigo–to the extent that she would crawl on her hands and knees to the bathroom. She was simply worn out from so many years of hard work. She had earned her rest.

One rainy December evening in 1966, Mother decided to walk to the nearby department store in Rensselaer. She made the mistake of not crossing at the intersection and the traffic was moderately heavy. The woman who ran her down simply didn't see her until it was too late. Mother, in her 71st year, barely made it to the hospital before she passed away.

The family sentiment: weren't we lucky to have had such a wonderful woman to guide us into our adult years.

Siblings

SISTER JANE

Whether it was because we were at the opposite end of the family spectrum or maybe because I was the *baby* of the family, somehow sister Betty Jane (whom we all called Janey) and I were always close. She had bright red hair and a diminutive frame, and she stood a little over five feet in height. She was attractive and had a fine sense of humor.

In her late teens, Janey was continuously surrounded by close friends. On summer weekends at the homestead, our diving platform at the bank of the Hudson River was usually shared by Janey and two or three of her girlfriends–and also a bevy of young male admirers who lived across the river. Janey was a great diver and also very competent at riding a surf board towed by an outboard motor boat.

She attracted several male admirers, sometimes dating more than one within a week. One was a doctor's son who lived across the river and was extremely egotistical. In the summer he wore white bathing suits, which amplified how well he was endowed. He was quite a physical specimen. I remember him once chopping a hole in the ice to take a brief swim one February day. Eventually, his self-esteem got in the way of the romance with my sister.

A variety of suitors came and went. It was hard keeping score. One was goofy, another drank too much and a third was gay. Quite a cast of characters.

My sister spent two years at Albany Business College, a private commercial institution. Uncle Will paid for it. He, too, doted on sister Jane because of her outgoing personality and probably because she was his only niece surrounded by a group of obstreperous nephews.

Uncle Will would take her by bus to a downtown Albany movie house and buy her ticket to a flick. She loved Bing Crosby. While Jane was safely enjoying the film, Uncle Will would go to a favorite bar across the street and have a few beers. After the movie, they would take the bus home together.

Janey read the music when playing the piano. She frequented downtown Albany's five-an-dime store, Kresge's (now K-Mart), where an elderly white haired African-American pianist would play any tune a prospective sheet music buyer wanted to hear. Over the years, she accumulated literally hundreds of sheet music selections. On Sundays, she would unfailingly carry an armload of sheet music along to the homestead. TV hadn't yet become available to the general public, so instead we often spent the evening singing around the piano as Jane played. When younger, I could really carry a tune, which served me well in later years while in the high school chorus and also singing as a tenor for forty years in the church choir.

I think those Sunday evenings of singing around the piano were a strong bonding influence between Janey and me. This Sunday evening music routine strongly reinforced my familiarity with the hit tunes of the late '30s and the early '40s. To this day, I recall the words to just about any hit song of that era, particularly if sung by the Andrews Sisters. When I think back over the years, I can't help but be convinced that those family and friend sessions on Sunday evenings were an amazingly fine way to spend the formative years.

Jane never liked driving a car, and in later life did it only by necessity. She would practice driving on the three-fourths-of-a-mile long dirt road approaching the homestead. After leaving the highway, the road crosses a swampy area before it passes between the fields on either side of the road. On one of her earliest attempts at driving, Jane turned right off the highway and then onto the dirt road which she managed to overshoot, thence plunging the car into the swampy stretch. We passengers simply gritted our teeth and held on tight. Miraculously, Jane kept driving through the swamp and somehow managed to get back onto the dirt road.

Why the Model A didn't tip over or at least get stuck in the swamp remains a mystery.

Although my sister never made much money at her challenging job as an office manager, she loved buying clothes, and shoes in particular. By far her favorite color was purple, another attribute that she and I shared. Her one extravagance was a mouton lamb coat. When Aunt Bess cooked fish for dinner, Jane would rush upstairs to ensure that her precious coat was hanging in the closet where it couldn't absorb the fishy fumes.

Janey was always fond of *naughty*–but never raunchy–stories and jokes and she would pass them on with glee once we were in our teen years.

After several years of dating, she settled on a tall good-looking neighborhood guy of German descent whose was a close high school colleague of brother Larry. Hans Dirzuweit had emigrated with his mom from Germany at age 9 and became a citizen when he joined the US Army in World War II. He was a brilliant chemical engineering graduate from Rensselaer Polytechnic Institute, introverted but increasingly sociable after a relaxing cocktail.

They were married at the Presbyterian Church in Rensselaer in a modest ceremony. Hans was in his Army uniform and sister Jane wore a purple hat, and purple suit with a purple blouse. She completed the ensemble with purple shoes. To me she looked beautiful.

After his stint serving in World War II, Hans returned home and began job hunting. He found a job readily enough, but it was at a paper mill in Tonawanda, near Buffalo, NY, some three hundred miles west and a five-hour drive from home. One of the saddest occasions of my life was attending Janey's final church service before she moved. The entire family was in tears, particularly my mother and I. It took a long time getting used to not having my sister nearby.

However, there was a bright side. On an annual basis, we would drive to Buffalo. Initially, these trips were made in the Model A Ford Roadster and it took an endless 11 hours. The interstate highway system was yet to be built. Invariably there were steep hills to be navigated, a boiling radiator, flat tires, etc. But we made it and it was fun to be together again.

Hans was a perfect host during our visits. He made sure we saw all of the interesting attractions in and around Buffalo: Niagara Falls, the zoo, Chrystal Beach (an amusement park on Lake Erie), the Twelve Apostles clock at the museum, the university, etc. When I went there as an eighteen-year-old high school senior with my closest friend along for the ride, Hans decided that we were old enough for a trip *on the town* which included my first alcoholic beverage: an Old Fashion (Southern Comfort) and an evening at the Palace, the last surviving burlesque theater in the state. Vaudeville acts and strippers galore–what a show! Sister Jane was disgusted with her husband for leading her youngest brother and his buddy astray.

While in Buffalo, Janey and Hans had two children, Tientje and Hans Staats Dirzuweit. Tientje was an old Dutch name Janey had gleaned from the birth lists of our ancient Dutch family Bible dating back to the early 1700s.

At the time of Tientje's birth, brother Bleecker was in the Navy stationed on Guam. Mother wrote to him in her notoriously bad penmanship to announce the new baby. Because the handwriting was practically illegible, Bleeck translated her writing as *Leekee Lu* and for two years he couldn't figure out why such a weird name was chosen. He finally straightened it out when he came home from the service. Tientje was the first of the 10th generation and was loved accordingly.

Hans was transferred home from Buffalo, and we were all pleased at the prospect of their return. For months before arriving, Jane would write her new slogan: *Back to the Sticks in 56.* They bought a small house in a neighborhood overlooking Rensselaer.

Jane was a good mother, albeit of the helicopter variety. She was always a steadying influence in our extended family and she maintained her sense of humor all of her life.

Her passing was tragic. Throughout her life she'd seldom been ill, experiencing the usual minor ailments such as colds and headaches. She was very active in the Rensselaer Presbyterian church governance, and one Sunday she was scheduled to make an announcement from the altar where the entire congregation could see and hear her clearly. She stood in front of the microphone, said a few words and then dropped to the floor. She was dead from an apparent brain aneurism at the age of 57. What a shock! There was no autopsy.

BROTHER LARRY

Larry, the oldest of my male siblings, was my idol. He had an outgoing personality with a great sense of humor and was always surrounded by friends. He was capable at just about any skill including carpentry, electrical work, mechanics, masonry and plumbing. He was a meticulous worker. He probably did more to improve the homestead than anyone else in its 300+ year history.

His entire life was replete with adventure. In his high school senior year, Larry built his own wooden boat, on the transom of which he mounted an outboard motor. The following summer, four buddies accompanied him in his small boat on a five-day trip to New York City via the Hudson River. Although they had some rainy weather and also some engine trouble, they made it. They saw some sights and slept in Central Park. Some went to Times Square and others enjoyed a game at Yankee Stadium. Returning home, in order to avoid burning fuel as well as mechanical problems, they hitched themselves to a tug-drawn barge heading north.

Adventure included spending most of his working life as an engineer on US merchant ships, sailing to Viet Nam during the war, the Middle East, Europe, Africa, Central America and along the coastal ports of the USA.

During World War II he briefly attended Dartmouth College with the aspiration of become a Navy pilot. He dropped out to serve on a PT boat in the Philippines.

After coming home from the service, Larry and brother Kim pooled their funds and bought out cousins who owned a share of the homestead. Following that, Larry equally distributed his ownership among my mother and his siblings and the other half of the property was solely owned by brother Kim.

Larry always had the academic ability to complete a degree but he delayed his college education until the age of 33. For a year he attended Massachusetts Institute of Technology (MIT) in Boston and later transferred to Worcester Technical Institute where he earned a BS in Mechanical Engineering. To partially finance this, he bussed tables at a diner.

After college, he went to sea spending just enough time away from home to earn sufficient funds to keep improving the house and to enjoy a new-found hobby:

skiing. There were romances over the years but he never married until he met a Norwegian shipping clerk named Torill while his ship was anchored for several months near the city of Alesund, Norway. Larry was 54 when he finally tied the knot.

In addition to being such an excellent worker, Larry was really a lot of fun. Over the years he brought home dozens of friends who were a treat to know, many of whom have remained close friends over these many years since Larry passed away.

Many of the characters he brought around could have been gleaned from central casting. An obnoxious barfly guest once accompanied a merchant marine colleague. She rudely criticized our care of the homestead and, by the time she departed the premises, we realized that her lack of manners, although appalling, were really quite funny.

Another visiting couple preferred to spend every day from noon on, consuming a stash of alcohol they always kept in a travel cooler. Two or three others had either done jail time or were headed in that direction. Another one was a brilliant physicist who brought around a parade of lovelies but couldn't kick his addictions which made him extremely argumentative.

For the main part, however, his guests were well traveled and most interesting.

Larry's humor was infectious. He often told hilarious stories about himself. I recall him telling about an incident which occurred when he was in the merchant marines with his ship anchored in South Korea. For some reason he had contracted an infection which had required daily shots in the butt for a week or so. For this he had to go ashore to an *urgent care* facility. He did this for a few days and in the process befriended several of the native Korean medical staff. He learned enough of the Korean language to have a buddy stencil *Good Morning* in Korean on his butt. When he next showed up at the facility, he dropped his drawers for the usual shot and the nurses saw the message. They enjoyed it so much that they called in the rest of the staff to join in the hilarity.

Brother Larry loved our brood of seven as well as their young friends. He maintained a stripped down 1930 ford Model A with no windshield and a wooden carrying box in which the kids would ride. He would drive them hurtling over the terrain of sand dunes, sapling trees and bumpy dirt roads in the area around the homestead. Although he was an extremely safe driver, the kids were terrified, but continuously asked for more.

Larry and the youngsters would take long exploratory walks along the banks of the Hudson, collecting driftwood for the fireplace and smashing glass bottles against rocks in those areas seldom visited by others. Although he was very strict about their behavior, he would often let them carry out their wildest fantasies: skipping flat rocks on the water surface, climbing trees, camping, catching fish and turtles, etc.

To this day, remembrance of *Uncle Larry* brings broad smiles to the now-grown youngsters.

Larry led a long and interesting life. Although unmarried until in his 50s, he and Torill brought up two fun-loving daughters and saw to it that they completed college. Monica, the oldest, became a teacher and Ingrid a talented artist. My oldest brother had an admirably long life span. While my parents and their generation passed on in their 60s or early 70s, Larry made it to age 85, finally succumbing to congestive heart failure even though he had two bouts with colon cancer within a few years of his death.

Brother Kim

He was born Joachim Peter Staats, the second son of six. Joachim is a biblical name appearing in family records since at least as far back as the 17th century. It was the also name of the second generation son responsible for the building of the homestead in 1696. The family called him *Kim* and, when he worked on the tugboats, he was often referred to as *Yock* (for Joachim).

Brother Kim, before he married, always had a small circle of friends. He was no scholar. He hated going to school and was occasionally obstreperous. He was preceded by academically inclined Janey and Larry and did not meet his teachers' expectations..

Although not academically inclined, Kim had amazing talent in the area of mechanics and could repair auto engines, diesel engines, and just about anything with mechanical parts. He was also excellent at home repair.

As a youngster, he loved the out of doors. He was particularly fond of camping trips in a huge metal-bodied lifeboat he rescued from the Hudson River Day Line. The boat was a visual atrocity. Kim built on a rugged cabin and then cut a recess in the hull into which he mounted an outboard motor. Camping trips were taken along the Hudson and would last two or three days. He would take along a couple of buddies and a brother or two.

Kim also like hunting–ducks, geese, turkeys, pheasants–whatever was in season.

Although more shy and retiring than older brother Larry, he was outgoing enough to court a young neighbor from across the river and became engaged while still in his teens.

Kim was quite young and needed Mother's written permission to go into the service. She reluctantly signed, realizing how much Kim hated school. This would give him a chance to mature, and he certainly did that, earning a GED (high school equivalency diploma) after leaving the Navy.

While in the Navy, Kim married Kay Snyder from across the Hudson. She traveled to San Francisco by train to be with him before he shipped out to sea. Kay loved the experience of being a war bride.

With capabilities similar to his older brother Larry, much physical improvement in the property took place in those post war years. Kim had a trench dug to the fresh water well, and, *voila,* we had running water. In the north wing of the house Kim installed a hot-water heater.

Initially, Kim used a gasoline-fueled generator for power, but he and Larry soon had electricity brought to the house. What an amazing difference it made to have electric lighting and appliances. While Larry installed wiring in the old section, Kim did the same for the north wing in which he and his wife, Kay, resided.

When first out of the Navy, Kim worked for an automotive repair business. Later on he went to work as a diesel engineer on the tugboats.

Living at the homestead was a very austere experience for Kim and Kay. While they had electricity, there was still no central heating. They had to rely on kerosene stoves. After some years, Kim and Kay bought a small modern home in Nassau and rented out the north wing of the homestead. They also bought a trailer on Sacandaga Lake, where they and their daughter, Sharon, would spend the warm weather months. For many years following their move to Nassau, we saw Kim and Kay and Sharon only occasionally. They had a new circle of friends and neighbors and our paths seldom crossed.

Tragically, Sharon became terminally ill with breast cancer. For a few years, she courageously fought the disease and used her time wisely to act as a resource person on the computer for cancer victims across the country, telling them what to expect and suggesting ways to cope.

Sharon had married and had two sons at the time of her passing at the age of 46. The boys were a godsend to brother Kim and Kay in their advancing years.

In their golden years, Kay's folks spent the winter at their Florida retirement park where they occupied a trailer. During those later years, I would make it a point to stop by on my winter month in the south. Kim and I would take long walks, making up for so many years of lost time. In the summertime we would renew our enjoyable visits by taking strolls or just engaging in lengthy conversations. It was so great to have him back with the family.

Kim began to suffer physical problems. He had a bypass operation and then, sadly, he contracted cancer. About five years before his passing, Kim came to spend more time with our family. We became very close in those final years. By the time he passed on in his late seventies, our renewed friendship had solidified.

BROTHER BARRY

Barent Schuyler Staats was the third boy born to my mom and dad. His sunny disposition was occasionally offset by a bad temper, particularly in his youth.

By the time he reached high school year he was one handsome dude, resembling swashbuckling Errol Flynn of movie fame. The girls fawned over him. He was so popular in high school that he was nominated to head the Student Council, a great honor. Unfortunately his politicking skills were woeful. His opponent was very adept in the political arena and in later years became mayor of Rensselaer.

Barry's buddy and campaign manager, George, tried his best but Barry simply wasn't marketable for that particular position. At the school campaign assembly when the two candidates presented their credentials to the entire high school student body, for some unknown reason Barry started off by imitating a well-known dullard dummy, Mortimer Snerd, invented by Edgar Bergen, a popular radio ventriloquist. "Howdy folks, hi y'all," he began.

"And there went dozens of votes." George later lamented. "It was over before it started."

There was a compensation, however. Later that year, Barry was elected president of the senior class, an esteemed achievement.

Barry graduated from high school in 1944, and shortly thereafter went into the Navy. By that time,

World War II was drawing to a close, so he spent his military career as a Yeoman stationed in Texas. Barry and I became very close. I think the strong friendship, which lasted some 80 years or so, started over Barry's choice in a lady friend. On leave from Texas, he brought home the photo of Anne, a girl he'd met down south. To me she had features resembling a boxer dog, and I let him know it by sending along a miniature ceramic boxer which was labeled *Anne*. By the time he received it, the romance had ended and he got a kick out of my gift. From then on, our relationship was smooth sailing.

Following his return from the service, brother Barry spent two years at Albany Business College, majoring in Accounting. He worked briefly in an Albany grocery store but soon realized the proprietor was a skin flint, paying all of 35 cents an hour. When he gave notice he was leaving, the old cheapskate short-changed him!

After that, he took a sales job at a classy men's store, where he befriended an older, somewhat horny guy names Les, who would go downstairs to the basement of the store and peer up through the heat register to look up the skirts of female customers.

Eventually, Barry found a job with Mobile Oil as an accounts manager, and there he stayed for several years. He spent some five years with a sweetheart of a girl named Audrey who, unfortunately, could best him in about any sport they engaged in together: croquet, softball, touch football, pool, etc. With his competitive nature, this rankled Barry. After so much time, Audrey's mother began to put the pressure on for an engagement, and my brother resisted the challenge and ended the relationship.

I have an interesting memory involving Audrey, one of the loveliest and most innocent girls I have ever known. For a diversion at the homestead, several of us would swim out in the Hudson River, with the goal of *hopping* a slow-moving sand barge pulled by a tug. We would horse around in the sand cargo for about a half hour and then dive off and swim to shore, and from there walk back to the homestead. It was a fun experience, but not without its risks.

Climbing aboard the barge, even though it was slow moving and very low in the water, was a challenging fete. Audrey, being such a good sport, joined us in a *barge-hopping* expedition one sunny summer afternoon. Did I forget to mention that the girl was physically very well endowed and could just barely be contained in the upper region of her bathing suit?

At any rate, Audrey's boarding the barge became a frantic challenge. Barry's best friend, Wil, stepped into the breach–literally. When she reached up he gave her a hand and helped haul her onto the barge deck. In the process, however, her right breast tumbled out of the swim suit and lay on the deck momentarily. Wil, not watching his feet, managed to step on the boob. In a few frantic seconds, she was safely on board with her body part tucked back in place.

Did Wil keep that little event secret? Of course not. Over a few beers he would often say, "Barry, no matter how well you get to know that girl, I'll bet you never get to step on her tit like I did!"

Brother Barry married a girl he met at work. Connie was often a fun person to be with. They had three children and lived in the town of West Sand Lake, NY. Like a good citizen, Barry became a volunteer firefighter. All went well until an alarm came in at 3 a.m. Connie urged him over and over to get up and get going. His only response (repeatedly): "Bite me in the ass!" Eventually he got up and answered the alarm–a false one.

Mobil Oil has a policy of rotating its personnel to a variety of locations and so the call came for Barry to move his family to Palmyra, New Jersey. Reluctantly they left the Capital District area of New York. They resided in Palmyra for several years but would return home for a vacation every year. Although we missed having Barry and Connie's family around and seeing them mature, they managed to do so without our vigilance.

When after a dozen years, the call came again from Mobil for him to move, Barry'd had enough and was done with being shuttled from place to place. He quit, sold some stock to maintain his family for a year, and moved back to the Albany, NY, area in 1968. Brother Barry then bought the north wing of the homestead from older brother, Kim. He and his family settled into their home, which included a half acre of land around the house donated to them by the rest of the homestead owners.

Barry's daughter, Kim, attended St. Rose College and also Syracuse University. She eventually moved to California and for a while worked in the pharmaceutical industry in San Francisco. Then she met and married Tom Lucas, a hard working horticulturalist who owned a few nursery sites, and they settled north of Los Angeles.

Daughter Cheryl worked for a while at a beauty spa. After having a son, Garrett, she took a job with a group of orthopedic doctors in Albany. Barry's son Randy, loved the world of musical entertainment, spent a few years in that career, but eventually settled in a computer design-related job in Saratoga, NY. He married and had two children, Emily and Barent, but the marriage didn't survive the professional musician years.

Barry was a physical *worker bee* at the homestead. He loved carpentry and lawn mowing. In his younger years he had been frugal. As he grew older he opened his wallet frequently to make improvements at the homestead. Although no golfer, he paid for a professionally-styled putting green for the enjoyment of others. It cost thousands. He bought a pricey pontoon boat and generously offered rides to anyone who was interested. He bought a small gazebo and located it on the hillside on his property overlooking the river.

One of Barry's most remarkable achievements was having a sizeable gazebo built on the family-owned riverbank on the Hudson. It is oval in shape measuring 18' by 13'. On a warm day, this is the gathering place for a peaceful afternoon overlooking the river. It has also served as a location for wedding ceremonies and for a bandstand at many other celebrations.

He was a visionary in terms of eye-appealing improvements. He extended the lawn area significantly, cutting down bushes and undergrowth to make large grassy expanses around the majestic walnut trees on the property. Eventually the lawn areas were extended to some three acres and more. This took joint efforts in mowing and weeding, but Barry pitched in with several others of us to keep the beautiful grounds in shape.

After leaving Mobil Corp., Brother Barry took a low-key job with the State of New York, proofreading legislative proposals. He loved the lack of pressure and could look forward to a pension from both the state and Mobil.

His life took a dramatic turn when he reached the age of 80. His wife, Connie, died around that time.

Barry cut loose from his usual routine and morphed into an outgoing party guy.

Unbelievable! He even became a *groupie* with a very popular, 8-person band, *The Refrigerators*. He would go dancing with daughter, Cheryl, once or twice a week. His preference as dance partners were blondes under the age of 40!

A particularly remembrance involves Brother Barry when in his 80s. One particularly hot, muggy summer day when he was alone in the downstairs of the north wing of the homestead, he decided to do some laundry. Perhaps because of the heat, he stripped naked before starting the task. As the washing machine was churning away, he looked out toward the river and observed a thunder storm suddenly coming out of nowhere. He became concerned for the two flags he always kept flying at the embankment overlooking the Hudson. The wind picked up to a gusty pace and Barry decided to go out and take down the flags–naked. Now as this wizened 83-year old was walking toward the river, a 60ish female guest was investigating the same storm from the porch of the old section of the house. Much to her amazement, she spotted Barry in the altogether taking down the flags.

When the guest came back into the homestead, she breathlessly announced, "You wouldn't believe what I just saw when I went out on the porch to check out the storm." Fortunately the family sense of humor carried the memory onward.

For several years, my octogenarian brother maintained this breath-taking pace. At age 87, however, his health began to fail and he passed on at age 88–after having enjoyed several years of amazing activity.

BROTHER GARY

Brother Gary died at age five before I was born, so I have no recollection of him at all. I know that he died from a strep germ he had incurred after visiting the hospital to treat severe burns. He had been playing with matches in bed and it proved to be a fatal mistake. Courageously my mother rowed across the river on a chilly November day because we had no telephone with which to call for help—but to no avail.

BROTHER BLEECK

Bleecker Breese Staats. That combination of old Dutch family names was bestowed on this boy who was undoubtedly the most unique of my brothers. From the outset, he was one of a kind with his amazing imagination and personality. I suspect that in modern terms he would have be classified as ADHD. His interests were extremely varied and deep. At an early age, he would talk incessantly about volcanos and dinosaurs. He always seemed restless and anxious to get involved in something different.

I was a few years younger than Bleeck, and we spent a great deal of time together in our youth. He knew how to push people's buttons and he was particularly adept at pushing mine. He would continuously tease me, calling me *glum* when I was in a sour mood (usually caused by himself). He also called me *roundy* because I had a round head. He would drive me to distraction, which also caused me to exhibit bizarre behavior. In one fit of fury, I can recall dashing his toy metal truck to pieces against the stone wall of the house. He immediately retaliated by smashing my favorite toy car, a green Packard, against the same wall. Of course I cried–that was his intent.

One time I soaked his favorite fluffy white toy dog in the chamber pot so thoroughly that it turned yellow. He fought back by squeezing my teddy bear's nose in and then letting go into a slow gastric emission while slowly releasing the nose. That, of course, caused the toy bear to smell repulsive every time I cuddled it to my chest.

I wasn't the only one Bleecker annoyed. I recall seeing brother Barry threatening him with an upraised croquet mallet. I can also see my mother chasing him down an alley with an axe in her hand. And there was the time he daringly stuck his tongue against the water pump handle on a frigid winter evening, and Sister Jane's beau d-jour threatened to pee on it to free him because Bleeck annoyed him as well. He even defecated in the bathtub when he heard that my future brother-in-law was coming to our house to take a bath because he was having plumbing problems at home.

When he was an early teenager and my temper tantrums were at their peak, Bleeck would goad me into life-threatening retaliations. When he cheated at croquet I chased him across the lawn, mallet raised and ready for the kill. When he teased me in the house, I grabbed a block of firewood and hurled it at him. Unfortunately I missed him as he ran into the pool room to escape my wrath. He then retrieved the block of wood and poised himself hidden in the stairwell in the pool room hall, knowing that I would soon come through the hall door. He then groaned as if he had been seriously hurt. Changing my emotions from hate to contrition, I rushed to Bleeck's assistance. As I came through the hall door, he brought that block of wood down onto my shoulders, sending me to the floor flat on my face. Of course I cried-that was always his intent.

In spite of those innumerable instances of battle, we remained close friends. We played together, swam together, tobogganed, slept together, and made up hypothetical dramas in which we would each played roles rather than taking a nap as directed.

Because his imagination was contagious, Bleeck was instrumental in broadening my horizons in the teen years. He maintained an aquarium of exotic fish. I recall that one Christmas I went to an Albany pet store to get him a rare tropical fish that he so desired for his collection. It was a cold winter day, and I waited an endless time for the bus to arrive and take me home. It was so cold that the fragile fish froze to death before I reached the house. Perplexed, I didn't know how to handle the problem but I knew that I didn't have the time or money to get a replacement. So I gave him the dead fish! He thought that was hilarious.

For a time he had a deep interest in classical music, an interest which he passed on to me. In those days, the records were Bakelite 12-inch disks played on a windup Victrola. He loved *Claire de Lune, Liebestraum* ballet music, opera, etc. What a broad and varied range of interests!

School was a bore to Bleeck. He just couldn't get interested in any courses and was frequently subjected to disciplinary action. He became a fixture in the principal's office because of fidgeting in class. I recall that he was directed to leave biology class because he kept playing with a 6" cube-shaped box. When the contents of the box were revealed, an ostrich egg appeared. Where Bleeck got it I'll never know, but it was enough to infuriate the teacher. During his high school years, six faculty out of a small group of 30 either retired or took a leave of absence. It could have been coincidental but I suspect Bleecker must have been a factor.

In playing games at home, he seemed constantly distracted. He was bored with cards and other board games of any kind. I've already mentioned how he drove Aunt Bess to distraction while playing *Pick Up Sticks*. He also took a toll on Uncle Will. When we played *Scrabble*, we would place the board on a lazy-susan so that it could be revolved as each player took his turn. The seven tiles were placed on a small wooden rack near the playing board. It seemed that Uncle Will had his rack of tiles too close to the board, so that if it was revolved slowly and carefully, the corner of board would scoop the tiles off of the rack and onto the floor. Bleeck's turn to play came just before Uncle Will's. Time and time again, Bleeck would give the damned board a good spin so that he could be facing the player area. The spin, in turn, would scoop my uncle's tiles onto the floor. After it happened the third time, Uncle Will stood up, scattering everyone's racks, tiles and the playing board onto the floor as he stalked out of the room, emitting a string of oaths which turned the air blue. As I said, Bleeck had a knack for rattling so many with whom he came in contact.

After high school, Bleeck took a job with a noted Albany photographer named Mr. Glen. Although the pay was minimal, my brother took a deep interest in working with a camera, an interest which he maintained all of his life. Of course he would relate his unique experiences. In a garret section of the studio, Bleeck found a small dust-encrusted window and opened it for fresh air. The ancient secretary told him that the window hadn't been opened in the 50 years she had worked there.

In another instance, Mr. Glen asked Bleeck to accompany him to the home of a very elderly dowager of Albany elite society. The proper lady wanted her photo taken with some antique furniture she had acquired. In the austere setting, a small fire was burning in the old brick fireplace. Bleeck's job was to arrange the setting to get the best photo. Mr. Glen suggested that the dowager might want to be stirring the fire to lend a more authentic aura. As she bent over to retrieve the poker, the old dear audibly passed gas. That set Bleeck trembling with mirth. Mr. Glen whispered in a threatening voice, "Bleecker, if you laugh, you're fired!" How Bleeck loved to tell and retell that story.

Bored by his routine at home and his low paying job in Albany, Bleeck joined the Navy in 1948. He served with the occupying American forces on Guam for two years. The long, rough, voyage to the remote Pacific island took its toll. Seasickness gripped Bleeck and he suffered. He made the decision to give up eating solid food altogether until reaching Gaum. This worked for three days, until hunger pangs overcame him as he passed though the bakery department of the galley. Feasting his eyes on raw dough being readied for making donuts, he no longer could resist the temptation.

"I scooped up handful after handful of the raw dough and stuffed it into my mouth," he recalled. "It tasted w-o-n-d-e-r-f-u-l! Within a few hours my stomach began to churn. I rushed to my bunk where the heaving commenced. It went on and on with my stomach churning endlessly. I stayed right in the bunk for several days until the seasickness had subsided. It was the most physically painful experience of my young life. By the time I recovered, we had reached Guam. From then on for two years all went well."

On Guam, Bleeck had the opportunity to take advantage of his newly-found interest in photography. He had a good camera. He experimented with tinted lenses, focusing, zooming over and over. One peak on the island was Mt. Tenjo which he frequently climbed in his free time. Bleeck took hundreds and hundreds of slides.

When Bleeck arrived home after two years in the Navy, he treated us to slide shows of his two years on Guam. In spite of his photographic talent, seeing the same slides over and over and over soon wore thin. It became a family joke. One wag remarked, "It seemed we traveled to Guam every time it got dark."

We joked that insomniacs would flock to our doorstep to watch a boring rerun of slides that lulled them to sleep. People sometimes brought along restless children knowing that the slides would eventually cause their eyelids to droop.

Bleeck's return to civilian life was brief. He moved to New York City and took some menial jobs in photography, living in the YMCA. His standard of living was absolutely frugal. For a while he was trying to live on vitamin pills!

Bleeck was never a good money manager. I can recall that once he used part of his meager earnings to buy a ceramic human skull that lit up in the dark!

He never had a steady girlfriend and once in a while he would bring home a prospective partner who, we were all convinced, was on board just because he needed someone along to carry his photographic equipment.

Eventually the lure of stability prevailed and Bleeck joined the US Coast Guard for a four-year stint. He received a subsistence-and-quarters allowance to rent an apartment in Jersey City with several other Coast Guard servicemen. Those years were fun times for me because Jersey City was within commuting distance to the big city. We could use his spare bed or rent an unoccupied apartment from his loveable old landlady, Mrs. Egan, who looked over her brood of military tenants like a mother hen.

Bleeck's social life took an upturn. With a few buddies to share an apartment, the fun began. I recall a story he told of a torrid romance one his roommates was having, and then something she had done culminated the relationship. To show his disdain for his former girlfriend, he pasted her portrait photo down in the apartment toilet bowl where the group practiced their urinating expertise using her face as a target. A few weeks later, the romance resumed. To celebrate, he invited the old girlfriend to a party at the apartment. Unfortunately, he neglected to detach the photo from the toilet bowl. When the girlfriend went into the toilet she saw the placement of her photo. This time around, the romance ended for good.

Bleeck was always gregarious–he made close friends quickly. As a consequence, he would invite a buddy or two home for weekends. My best buddy was going with a girl, Ronnie, who had moved to Albany to attend college and was staying at the YWCA. She had a ready supply of girlfriends to arrange dates for the Coast Guardsmen who came into the area. She was very selective about the guys and girls she coupled. A group of us would go square dancing on Saturday nights, and this arrangement went on for several months.

Once in a while there were mismatches. Bleeck brought home a guy named Murray, a polite, good looking young man in his 20's with a fine sense of humor. Ronnie was a little doubtful about a YWCA friend, Lily, who had a reputation for being overly flirtatious. The girl had been dropped by a number of prospective suitors because of her aggressive nature. She was pretty with a fine figure, but underneath that fine-looking surface was this secret flaw.

Ronnie coached her on several occasions. "Lily, you have to take it slowly. Nice guys don't want a girl to come onto them suddenly. It might result in a one-night stand, but then he'll drop you and that's the last you'll see of him." They rehearsed and rehearsed for the forthcoming date.

It just so happened that my girlfriend, Evie, and I rode in the backseat of Murray's car when the double date finally came off. Having listened to Ronnie's concerns, I was apprehensive about Lily's behavior. Lily got into the passenger side of the front seat–and immediately slid over so that her leg was touching Murray's.

"Boy, you sure are a good-looking one," she effervesced. From then on her behavior went downhill, but it was downright hilarious for both my date and me.

"Turn on the radio," Lily suggested. "Let's have some tunes." He did as suggested and Lily began singing along with a familiar song she knew. Unfortunately, her voice was far off key and much too loud. The situation had Murray (who had been forewarned), Evie and I in stitches. So much so that there were tears in our eyes. Lily, oblivious to our laughter, continued belting out the song and it seemed her voice became more and more dissonant.

Her next action was to snuggle into Murray's shoulder as he was driving, kissing him on the neck in the process. He furtively attempted to contain her amorous behavior, pleading, "Could you please back off, you're breathing on my carnation!" He was only citing the carnation in an attempt to get her to give him some room–there was no flower attached to his lapel. "I don't see any carnation!" she responded and once again, the other three of us dissolved into peels of mirth. It was a long evening but we enjoyed the outing for reasons other than just the dancing and refreshments.

Eventually the time came to fix Bleeck up on a date and Evie was able to persuade a nurse friend to go out with him. Once again, I was apprehensive. This time I was just afraid Bleeck would say something offensive, or maybe neglect the girl if he didn't find her attractive. Evie and I were in the front seat of my car and we drove to Evie's friend Doris's apartment to pick her up. Naturally, we were curious to see how the relationship would develop and both Evie and I took turns looking in the rearview mirror to keep an eye on what transpired. At first Bleeck and Doris engaged into politely guarded conversation.

We went square dancing and had a fine time engaging in that strenuous activity as well as enjoying liquid refreshments and sandwiches. It developed into a fine, fun evening.

On the way home, the romance between Bleeck and Doris took a torrid turn from what we could see in the rear view mirror. Polite conversation had been upgraded to wild, passionate kissing. What a change of pace! Evie and I were both pleased that there was a mutual attraction between Doris, who could be serious and determined, and Bleeck, who was inclined to be unpredictable.

We were hoping that there would be future double dates, but after that fling Bleeck didn't bother to contact Doris. Several months later, he must have had a guilty conscience, because he sent Doris a Christmas card reading only, "I'm sorry." One year later, he received a return card from Doris at Christmastime, "What are you sorry about?" she wrote. They immediately resumed dating and in six months they were married.

By the time he married, brother Bleeck had left the Coast Guard at the end of his tour of duty, and returned to civilian life. He took a job as a freight rating clerk with IBM in Dutchess County. The marriage produced four children. Our families never drifted very far apart because we enjoyed each other's company, and our children were very close in age. Bleeck and Doris would take some of our brood for a week or so in the summertime and we would reciprocate.

Their eldest daughter, Maelene made a career of nursing. The eldest son, Chip, became a family counselor and is living in Kansas, married to a teacher, and is the father of four fine children. Son Pieter is a whiz of a mechanic on a large farm and has a lovely wife and two sons. Daughter Amanda is a librarian with five outgoing and talented offspring.

And so the Staats line continues to thrive!

Bleeck, like Aunt Bess, seemed always to be in good spirits in spite of things that may have depressed someone else. His and Doris' combined work-related income was just enough to afford their cramped, development house and their sizeable family of six. To me, the house was depressing. It was small, with no basement and with linoleum tiles peeling off the floor. But to Bleeck, it was a palace. He planted trees in the back yard and out front.

After several years, he and Doris accumulated enough to buy an old farmhouse on the other side of town. It needed a lot of work and Bleeck wasn't handy or interested in carpentry, electrical work, plumbing, etc. But it was home and they loved it.

Hiking in the Catskill mountains became Bleeck's passion away from home. He also became a bird enthusiast. In place of his previous obsession with volcanos and dinosaurs, birds took center stage. And, as usual, Bleeck's enthusiasm had to be shared with family and friends.

We were all introduced to photos of birds and were *forced* to imitate bird calls. When walking in the woods, Bleeck would often cock his head upon hearing a bird call. "That's a yellowbellied sapsucker!" he would expound.

In advanced years, he initiated a hiking group for aging friends. They called themselves *Bleecker's Creepers* and their favorite terrain was the Catskills. They hiked in all seasons.

Hiking was Bleeck's physical undoing. With so much energy he climbed every one of the Catsikll's high peaks (3,500 feet or more) over a period of years.

At work, after a strenuous weekend, he experienced a debilitating heart attack. He was undaunted, however. Within a few months he was again climbing his beloved Catskills. After the heart attack, he again managed to scale every one of the highest peaks.

Doris died from heart failure in November of 1992 at the age of 61. She was an addicted smoker most of her adult life. To keep himself occupied, Bleeck continued on with his mountain-climbing expeditions. Two years after Doris' passing, he felt a tightness in his back which he attributed to having his backpack too tight. The pain continued to annoy him for several days and he began seeing a chiropractor. Still the pain continued. A few more months passed, and a friend persuaded him to see a medical doctor.

The diagnosis was terminal cancer. Bleeck had been suffering from prostate cancer for months. By the time he sought medical help it had metastasized into his spinal column. He was in stage four and had only a short while to live. The final weeks were pure agony. His doctor limited his use of morphine and other pain killers and he would be racked with pain for hours on end. Finally the end came at the age of 65.

Those who came in contact with brother Bleeck will never forget him. He had boundless energy and interests. He could be irrepressible and obstreperous. He could get under your skin, but you had to love this most unusual character.

A Partner for Life-Sandy

Grace and wisdom and luck were there in full force when I met Sandy Reimann. I was 22 and she was 18. Our paths crossed without incident several times because she was the younger sister of a friend, Bill Reimann. I had been seeing one or two girls, but none were serious relationships in spite of the fact that I was looking for someone permanent. Several of my close friends had already married and I envied their new life style.

In May of 1955, Bill Reimann married his high school sweetheart, Marcia Smith. Sandy and I were both wedding attendants. Some weeks after the wedding she accepted my invitation for a date. We went horseback riding with Bill and Marcia on a lovely autumn day. It was a fun experience. Her horse trotted just ahead of mine and it commenced to pass gas. Loudly. Often. Having grown up in a family of boys with scatological leanings, I thought this was hilarious.

I think the humor was due to my mother and aunt calling us *barbarians* for breaking wind–and many very young guys enjoy the reputation of being barbaric. I watched Sandy and noticed her shoulder shaking from laughter. Apparently, she was enjoying the horse's *indiscretion* as much as I.

Sandy readily accepted a second date followed by a third. Thence followed two years of seeing each other exclusively. We went on many double dates, attended a lot of social events, enjoyed travel, concerts, sports, and mostly being alone together for quiet times at the homestead.

By October, 1956 I made up my mind to marry her. We mutually agreed it was time to tie the knot. I so clearly recall asking her dad for her hand in marriage. She and I had been playing tennis with friends. When we got back to her house, I sprinted upstairs where her father was tying his shoes after awaking from a nap.

"I want to marry your daughter!" I breathlessly announced. He thought a moment and then responded, "Do you think you can teach her to turn off the lights in the daytime?" We had a great life together, but, come to think of it, I never could get her to turn off the lights when it was broad daylight outside.

We married in June of 1957. Our plan was to stay overnight in the Albany area so that I could attend my Masters' Degree graduation ceremony the next day. After the wedding at First Church in Albany, we had the reception at the downtown Ten Eyck hotel. It was a hot, muggy day and the thermometer zoomed up to 95 degrees. Incredibly, the hotel air conditioning system was out of order. It was insufferably hot on the dance floor. I had a diversion, however, when two of Sandy's young nephews joined me at the balcony to drop off full glasses of water onto the empty parking lot nine stories below.

I had borrowed brother Larry's car for a getaway vehicle fearing mine would be booby trapped.

When the reception ended, Sandy and I hastily decided to avoid the graduation ceremony and to head for Lake Winnipesaukee where I had rented a lakeside cabin. We would spend the first night of our honeymoon in Vermont. Ours was an ideal honeymoon–billing and cooing, swimming, eating out and sightseeing–including a mail packet boat ride on the lake. The weather was perfect.

We took the long way back home, stopping overnight to spend time with Bill and Marcia at Hampton Beach, New Hampshire, and then traveling on through northern Maine, New Hampshire and Vermont. We spent two nights with Sandy's sister's family who ran a dairy farm in Canton, New York.

Sandy had a secretarial job with an architect firm and I started my teaching job at Hudson High School in September. Although he commended Sandy's fine work, her boss let her go on the basis that she would soon be taking off time to have children. Back then he could get away with that, but surely not today!

We rented my mother's upstairs apartment and enjoyed the blissful adjustment to married life. Money was scarce so we entertained by serving tuna casserole dinners and then playing pinochle. We seldom ate out. Sandy had taken a part time waitress job. She never complained about spending long hours on her feet, low tips, or late evening hours. Toward the end of 1958, son Mark arrived. He was an exceptionally quiet, undemanding baby. Sandy became an ideal mother.

Eleven months later, son Grant arrived. He, too, had an easygoing disposition. We experienced a more relaxed attitude toward the second baby, fretting less about him and taking fewer photos

We acquired a Great Dane dog. Our quarters became too cramped so we rented brother Kim's north wing of the homestead. Living conditions were Spartan--cramped kitchen, kerosene stoves, muddy driveways in wet weather. We had only one neighbor. Sandy seldom complained even though our cars were clunkers.

In 1961 daughter Jennifer arrived. She was a bit more testy than the boys but by that time we'd adjusted to having a family. Two years later, daughter Kristina (Giss) arrived. She just slept, enjoyed her food and smiled for two years. We worried that by two she wasn't walking, but the doctor assured us that she would eventually get the energy to get up on her feet. At age 3, his prediction came true.

All this time, Sandy was a perfect partner. Three more children came our way. Sandy and I seldom quarreled and when we did, most of the time the problem was my doing.

What a fine treasure I had married! Sandy was an excellent cook and housekeeper and flower gardener. While she was a caring mother, she was no pushover. If our children missed their curfew, she went out looking for them. Bad behavior wasn't tolerated.

In her fifties, Sandy became a professional care giver. For some time she worked as a nursing home administrator–but the pay didn't nearly compensate for the hours she put in. After the nursing home, Sandy took on several local home-care jobs. Generally, these jobs were with old people who were terminally ill.

Some were challenging. There were two maiden lady sisters who had very rigid ideas. For instance, when daylight savings time occurred, they would get up and go around the house changing the clocks at 2 a.m. rather than wait until morning. "Two in the morning is when the weatherman said the time changes and we think it's best to change the clocks then," they stubbornly affirmed.

Over the years since Sandy passed away, I still receive compliments about how caring she was. She would be saddened, however, every time she lost a patient to the grim reaper.

Although quiet, she had a sense of humor. There was that time we were staying at a motel in colonial Williamsburg. We were out in the parking lot on our way to the historic site when I suddenly remembered that I left my wallet back in the room. I was smoking a cigar at the time. While I was inside the motel fire alarm went off–in the elevator the cigar smoke had triggered it. Sandy looked on from the parking lot as the motel was evacuated. One woman asked her, "I wonder what set off the alarm?" "I'm not sure, but it probably had something to do with my husband!" Sandy responded.

She thoroughly enjoyed our cultural outings–plays, concerts and the opera in particular. Her favorite opera was "Madam Butterfly;" mine was "Rigoletto." We did a lot of traveling together. In the United States our favorite park, known for its beauty, was Yosemite in California. Our favorite excursions were to Lexington, KY, horse country and also to Natchez where we loved to visit the plantation homes when they were open to the public. Newport, RI, was another favorite as was Savannah, GA. Outside of this country, we toured Europe in a travel van with all of the family on board. We flew to South America where we mostly enjoyed Rio de Janeiro and Machu Picchu. There were also trips to Hawaii, Tahiti, Australia and New Zealand.

She was drawn to playing the slots at casinos. She usually came out ahead—while I consistently lost. We found ourselves gambling in Saratoga, Connecticut,

Las Vegas, Atlantic City and even Puente del Este in Uruguay and a place near Vienna, Austria. When in Austria I expressed my frustration after yet another losing evening. Her suggestion: "Change your approach. You flit from one machine to another. Do what I do and stick with one machine the whole time."

I followed her advice—and wound up losing once again. When I grumbled, she huffed, "And I suppose you're going to blame me for that." There was no winning with that lady.

Our marriage wasn't trouble free. We each had our own identities and we jealously guarded our individuality. For instance, after putting up with my penchant for cars that were *clunkers,* she went out and bought a new one for herself. "It's my own money and I chose to use it as I please," she upbraided me. In 1992 I came home to find a **FOR SALE** sign on the front lawn. I knew nothing about it but she had decided that it was time to move because the house was too big and needed pricey repairs. The children had matured and moved out. She didn't tell me about it because she knew I would give her flack. Now, that's independence!

Selling the big house and moving into a newer town house in the suburbs was one of the best moves we had ever made. Two bedrooms, new appliances, and smaller living quarters made for more sensible living. We were wrong about one thing, however. We thought we'd seen the last of sharing the house with the offspring—but daughter Giss and her husband, two young sons and a huge dog came to stay with us while their new home was being built nearby. Over the several months they were with us, we never had as much as one run in.

Sandy had little patience with my drinking. There was that New Years Eve party when we decided to drive in separate vehicles—me in my pickup truck and her in the sedan. She left after midnight and I stayed on to sip a few with Beaky Graham. When I finally decided to drive home, I drove my truck into an orchard and got it stuck in the snow. Rather than freeze on a frigid night, I staggered back to Beaky's house about a mile away from the orchard and spent the night there. The following morning, he used his truck to pull me out of the orchard. In the meantime the farmer who owned the orchard had phoned the state police to complain about my truck. When the police phoned looking for me, Sandy suggested "When you catch up with him, why don't you put him in jail for a very long time."

When my wife reached her 60s, she decided to winter for a few months in Florida at a mobile home retirement park. I wouldn't join her because of part time teaching obligations and also the church choir and treasurer's responsibilities.

When we talked about it, I said, "I won't be joining you," citing my commitments. Her response? "Who asked you?"

I did, however, find a week or so to join her. We took walks, lounged around the community pool and even drove to Key West.

Ovarian cancer came upon Sandy while she was in Florida. The disease silently takes over with no warning signs. By the time it was discovered, the damage was done: Sandy was in the fourth stage of terminal cancer. She suffered for several months from the cancer and from the chemo treatment after-effects. Eventually we called hospice and by October she was gone.

Life hasn't been the same since I became a widower, but I am so grateful for the 47 years we shared as man and wife.

THE NORTH COUNTRY CONNECTION

When I married Sandy, I became a part of a family connection in upstate New York's St. Lawrence County. Her half-sister, Jean, was one of the most admirable people ever to become a close friend. She and her husband, Stan, had developed a family who became friends for life.

Life wasn't easy for Jean as a teenager. She was brought up in Rensselaer County. Her folks had split, she was married and had a daughter while still in her teens. Her husband was killed at work in a motor vehicle accident. It was at the beginning of World War II and to make ends meet, Jean took a job at General Electric Company in Schenectady where she met Stan

Thompson and they soon developed a relationship. Tragically, Stan's brother, Warren, who was to inherit the family dairy farm in Canton, New York, was also killed in an accident and Stan, who was an aspiring electrician, hesitantly took over in assisting his dad run the dairy farm. He and Jean and her daughter, Judy, moved to Canton. I met Jean and Stan and their young family one summer in the '50s while they were camping at Fish Creek camp site in the Adirondacks. It was mutual liking on both sides. Jean and Stan were outgoing and down to earth.

In 1957 Sandy and I married and spent on overnight with Jean and Stan and family in the final days of our honeymoon.

In the 1970's the Thompsons bought land on the banks of the Upper Saranac Lake and the entire family pitched in to build a 5-bedroom camp. From then on, my family counted the days when we could spend time in the North Country.

Stan and Jean brought four sons into the world—Larry (who became a truck driver), Dan (a computer whiz), Rick (an expert mechanic) and David (another computer guy). They blended so well with our seven youngsters and we never had to worry about adverse relationships. After all, the summer camp offered everything growing children would enjoy—boating, swimming, water skiing, fireside fun in the evening—with no TV or smart phones for distraction.

Sandy and I would share in the expense of food and fuel (for the boats). We also would share in the labor by splitting firewood, cleanup and assistance with food preparation.

During the year we would sometimes share in family events, such as dinners and weddings. Upon occasion, we would make excursions to the North Country to enjoy snowmobiling and winter fun.

When they matured, it was fun to share our social lives with the Thompsons. Rick and I became close companions—with him often coming to Rensselaer for a weekend of socializing. Larry, Dan and Rick married and had children. David led a bachelor's life until his 50s.

Jean's daughter, Judy, became a school teacher and later an education supervisor and eventually an historian for the village of Canton before her retirement.

Stan died of cancer when only 72 and Jean passed away at age 80. The camp was sold not long after Jean's passing but Rick and David continued to rent cabins on Fish Creek every summer. Sadly, Rick died from cancer in his early 60s, leaving behind a son and a grandson and a daughter.

The relationship with the Thompson family continues as my offspring and I will not let it die even though circumstances change as time goes on.

Offspring

MARK

Exploring our family tree could be an endless endeavor. Sandy and I had seven offspring and just keeping track of them has been a challenge. In the interest of time and needless ramblings, I will confine most of the tenth generation discussion to my immediate family.

Son Mark was the first to arrive on the scene. We were living in the upstairs apartment over my mother at the time and were enthusiastic and well prepared for the arrival. He was born Mark Lawrence Staats at Brady Hospital, a Catholic Diocese institution famous for its care of newborns. Mark was a well-behaved baby who, throughout his life remained bright, easy going and considerate.

There were, of course, minor incidents that can't escape memory, like the time he spent locked up in the city jail. It seems he and a few teenaged friends were spending their idle time pelting snowballs at passing vehicles. Mark had good aim and thought it was a harmless pastime. Unfortunately the local police didn't agree when a well-directed missile hit the windshield of the patrol car. When the vehicle screeched to a halt, his companions scattered, but Mark held his ground. He later told us that the snowball *he* threw did not hit the police car–and just how were they to know that? When questioned by the police, he answered with a nervous grin on his face that would without doubt read *guilty as charged*. That grin he'd developed early on in life whenever he was being reprimanded.

And so he was given the full treatment: hands cuffed behind his back, a firm officer's hand pushing his head down as he was guided into the back seat–the whole ball of wax. He was remanded to a cell containing one other prisoner. The single phone call was placed, and soon his mother and I were at the police station.

Fortunately, the police were in a benevolent mood and released him to our custody with a mild reprimand. The $75 fine was paid out of money saved on his newspaper delivery route.

Memories! In his teen years, Mark loved to sleep, especially past the noon hour. I recall needing him to help me with some task, so I went to his bedroom and shook him awake–at 1:30 in the afternoon! Groggily, he sat up in bed and muttered, "Anything I hate is having someone ruin my day by waking me up early!"

Mark graduated from high school with honors. Since his next younger brother was soon to follow, I took the opportunity to treat them in joining me for a round-the-world tour which started off with a four-month teaching assignment in Melbourne, Australia, followed by stopovers in Indonesia, Sri Lanka, Egypt, and Greece. In Luxembourg, we were joined by Sandy and the five other children to spend a month visiting Germany, France, England, Norway, Denmark and Iceland. It was a dream experience for me and the older children, but a nightmare at times for Sandy. She had all of the chores imaginable traveling with our family in an extremely cramped RV.

Throughout the trip Mark was an exemplary traveling companion–except for that instance in Athens when he disappeared for a few hours in the Plaka where we were staying.

"I forgot where we were heading and wandered into a side street," he explained.

Following the trip, Mark and Grant both joined the Navy. Grant took to it with such dedication that he made it a career as an officer in the US Navy SEALS. Mark didn't enjoy it at all, especially after completing boot camp. He was assigned to a rusting ship in the Charleston, SC, Navy Yard where he faced some months of galley duty–scrubbing pots and pans and serving meals.

Uncharacteristically, my oldest son abandoned his obligations and went AWOL. His tearful phone call home resulted in his mother and I suggesting he contact his recruiting officer with whom we'd been friends for a number of years.

If Mark was looking for sympathy he called the wrong person. The Navy recruiting officer admonished him, "For Christ Sake, stop being a baby and get your sorry ass back to the Goddamned ship. I'll call them and let them know you are coming!" Mark bit the bullet and received only a minor reprimand. Later he was stationed aboard a sub tender in Sardinia and was much happier with that tour of duty.

Following the Navy, he spent two years at the local community college and later received his four-year degree from Siena College, thanks to money put aside while in the Navy.

Forgetfulness or just not concentrating has plagued Mark during his adult years. Locking his keys in his car is a typical example. At the two year college, it would happen at least once a week. He'd have to contact a security guard to bail him out. Over time, he and the guard became friends because of their continuous contact.

When he transferred to the four year college, things didn't change. It was a different campus and a different vehicle, but the locking problem followed him without fail. During his first week on the new college campus, Mark locked his keys in his car.

He contacted the new security guard: "My name is Mark Staats and I've locked my keys in my car. Please remember this face because I will be contacting you repeatedly with the same problem." That set the tone.

Shortly after college Mark married and had two children, Meghan and Kevin, who grew up to be exemplary offspring. The marriage didn't work out. Mark had met his wife on an internet dating service and has continued with that method of finding a partner.

His first attempt at online dating was disappointing. He'd arranged to meet the prospect at a local eatery. He drove into the parking lot and waited for the car described by a young lady who seemed like a dream come true on his internet contact. When the expected date arrived and her car pulled into the parking lot, Mark was dismayed. He could see this massive hulk of a figure which seemingly filled the entire front seat.

"What did you do about that?" I interjected as he later described the encounter to his mother and me.

"I started my car and drove away," he responded.

Mark and I took one side of the ensuing disagreement about his course of action while his mother took the opposite side.

"That wasn't very polite," his mother argued. "You could have at least treated the young lady to dinner."

"Mom, why would I build false hopes in a relationship that I knew was going nowhere." I agreed. That, of course didn't change Sandy's mind.

Mark, the most easygoing of the seven offspring, remarried and later remarried again. This time he hit pay dirt with a lovely, quiet young lady much more suited to his personality.

Over the years, I've observed an interesting phenomena regarding my offspring as well as several others their age. *Most of the divorces were followed by very successful second marriages. In thinking about it I conclude that immature decision making by both partners caused the first marriage to fail.*

After trying out a couple of different jobs, Mark was hired by the great State of New York as a collector of delinquent sales taxes. He sure had some interesting stories regarding the collection process. At first, he made the contacts by telephone but later, accompanied by two others, he did the contacting in person.

Previous to making personal or phone contacts, the state would send several collection letters to the delinquent taxpayer. Each letter would be more threatening than the last. The phone responses were often argumentative.

In one instance, Mark contacted a man who had owed more than $5,000 in back taxes for some time and had not responded to any previous written communication. When Mark talked to him, the guy went on the offensive: "Does the state happen to know that I've been unemployed for more than two years?" he demanded to know. "Yes," Mark answered calmly. "We also know that you recently bought a brand new Peugeot, a luxury car worth several thousand dollars."

This was followed by a few moments of total silence at the other end of the line. And then the guy said, "Does the state happen to have an installment plan for repayment?" He caved.

When it came to in-person collections, the encounters could become scary. The usual process would be for two or three state sales-tax representatives to arrive at the business location, commandeer cash register tapes and then close the place down. Remember, this would be after the state had made several previous attempts without results. Belligerence was sure to be in the air. Often the person manning the cash register was only an employee caught in the middle.

One tax delinquent had a unique way of handling the situation when he found the state was approaching his doorstep. He phoned the local sheriff and said, "There are a couple of guys on their way here to bully me and I need protection. Be sure to bring your pistol!"

When Mark and his colleague arrived, the sheriff appeared and demanded that the state collectors raise their hands in the air and stand against the outside wall of the business establishment. Mark used his cell phone to contact the local state police office and soon they arrived to diffuse the situation. It may have been all in a day's work, but it sure concerned me that Mark was sometimes involved in potentially threatening situations. Fortunately, they were few and far between.

Of all of the seven children, Mark was the only sports nut. It must have come from my brother Barry, the only one of my siblings who was interested in sports. In baseball Barry backed Cleveland and hated the Yankees. Other sports didn't interest my brother, but son Mark had strong interests in both baseball and football.

In a way, I admired Mark's deep interest in sports. It enabled him to engage in intensely interesting conversations with relatives and visiting friends with whom he had little else in common. Mark also followed the political scene closely, which was more down my alley. I am a social conservative but Mark leaned further to the right and is more deeply firm in his convictions. It makes for interesting and spirited interaction.

GRANT

Our second child was also a son, Grant Schuyler Staats. I was overcome with delight. Having grown up in a family of several boys, I thought of the fun and companionship the two sons, only eleven months apart, would have. As usual, the second child was cared for in a much more relaxed manner than the first. We had learned the ropes of first born parenthood and were less uptight with the second.

Grant developed a temporary lisp when he first began to talk. He apparently did a lot of thinking about things that perplexed him. There was that curious question about the tooth fairy. After losing two or three teeth, which were put under his pillow with the assurance that he would be visited by the tooth fairy, he expressed concern in that lisping style of talking. "Can the tooth fairy thmell teeth?" he inquired.

"I really don't know, but why do you ask?" I responded.

"Well, the tooth fairy always comesh at night when ith's dark. He can't sthee the teeth in the dark stho he mustht be able to sthmell 'em." That was an early clue to his inquiring nature.

Both boys were good in school, but Mark was more academically inclined, and Grant was much more practical. Early on, I observed Mark's practical limitations. I was once doing some carpentry work and asked him to bring me a two-by-four strut about five feet long. He came to the doorway holding the wood horizontally. He couldn't get through the door until I told him to turn the strut to a vertical position. Grant, however, developed considerable skill at carpentry, plumbing, electricity and mechanics. Mark recognized that he was hopeless at these skills but he willingly helped in several other ways–mowing lawns, shoveling snow, maintaining the compost toilet, removing trash, fireplace preparation, wood-stacking, etc.

Both sons were terrific traveling companions, particularly during the four months we spent in Melbourne, Australia. We stayed with the Hulls family whom Sandy and I had befriended 12 years earlier when I had taken a one-year leave of absence to teach at the Royal Melbourne Institute of Technology. At that time, the Hulls offspring were small children, as were ours, but to me it was amazing how well they got along. By 1978, all of the children had grown into their late teens. The Hulls made room for us to live with them during the weekdays and on weekends Mark, Grant and I would drive some 50 miles to the Hulls' summer vacation cottage on the Mornington Peninsula.

Both boys enjoyed tennis and both were interested in an atrocious-sounding band which Richard Hulls had formed. The friendships included the other three band members, which made my sons' Australian stopover much more enjoyable. On the weekends, our small family gorged ourselves on fast foods and fish and chips. During the week Elizabeth Hulls prepared wholesome meals.

Upon return to the USA both Mark and Grant went into the Navy for three-year stints. Then both Mark and Grant attended Hudson Valley Community College. Grant steered toward electronics and Mark chose business. Mark severed his relationship with the military, but Grant chose to remain as a reservist.

Grant left home to travel to Coronado, California to take his *BUD/S* training in preparation of become a Navy SEAL. With his determination, athletic ability (particularly swimming) and congenial personality, he succeeded. He maintained his status as a reservist and went on to complete a BS majoring in electronics at SUNY Utica/Rome Institute of Technology, an upper division college.

Grant married and had two sons, Ethan and Evan. His young wife realized she had mistakenly made a commitment too young in life to a husband who was often on duty away from home. Grant remarried–a lovely attractive blond who had also been married and had three sons. To their credit, both Grant and his wife worked closely with their prior spouses in bringing up their children. Grant's first wife and her family have remained close friends for decades.

In recent years Grant, who now had more than 30 years of service, has been promoted to Captain, a most praiseworthy achievement.

JENNIFER

While dealing mostly with boys all my life, it was a change of pace to have a baby girl, Jennifer Anne, come into the family. Both Sandy and I had agreed to name her Evelyn after Sandy's aunt who died when in her 20s. Ah, but there was a hitch. Previously I had spent two years with a former sweetheart named Evelyn, and we were afraid tongues would wag if we named our new offspring after an old flame. So our second choice, Jennifer, it was.

Bringing up a girl was a unique experience for us. In her very young years she was pampered with girlie things: dolls, feminine attire, etc., bestowed on her by her maternal grandmother. My mom was a *boys* person after mothering six of them.

Jenn was a loving daughter until those difficult teen years.

At about age 12, she became a real challenge with unpredictable mood swings and friends who required constant scrutiny. Her relationship with her two younger sisters was often tempestuous. I recall one frigid February day when Heather (daughter #3) had used her hair conditioner. As Heather awaited the school bus, Jenn followed her with a pitcher of water in her hand, determined to pour it on her sister's head. "Jenn," I shouted after her, "Get back here. It's frigid out and if you douse your sister, she'll turn to a pillar of ice." She backed down.

Eventually, she made it to maturity, when her mother and I could relax our vigil and enjoy our sweet daughter who seemingly had returned from the great beyond.

She married and had two sons, Zachary and Nicholas. As the years have passed, Jennifer has grown more and more self-assured. To me, it has been an amazing metamorphosis. Jennifer, in her youth, was very much of a follower, often spending time with some questionable companions. Since her twenties, she has become increasingly thoughtful and competent as well. In recent years, Jenn has been office manager for a very successful solar power firm employing some 50 people.

Jennifer took charge of younger brother Greg after he fell apart following his mother's death. He had long worked in the restaurant, a life style that, for him, led to alcoholism and experimentation with drugs. He paid little attention to his health and other important responsibilities. After hitting a particular low, daughter Jennifer stepped up to the plate and dealt with those issues which continued to plague him. By this time, he was deeply in debt involving back taxes and huge health costs. Jenn contacted social services and worked closely with them for the rest of Greg's life. She successfully arranged to have the vast majority of his debts forgiven. All of this required time and patience, but Jennifer persisted until the major problems had been eliminated.

My children have filled the gap left in my life after the loss of Sandy, my wife of 47 years. My daughters, in particular, have continuously looked after my welfare. Since son Greg, who shared my town house and cared for me for eight years, died unexpectedly at age 47, the girls have watched over me assiduously. I'm truly blessed. They will each phone several times a week and will often invite me to share dinner and other social events.

Although somewhat high spirited and meticulous to a fault, Jennifer remains loving and attentive. I'm so lucky that she lives close by.

Giss

Our family has often assigned nicknames that stuck for life. Daughter Giss, for instance was born Kristina Lynne Staats. Where on earth did the appellation, "Giss" come from I can't recall. She prefers it, but also enjoys being called "Lulu" which is probably associated with her middle name.

Giss is one of kind. Since early childhood he has been strong-willed and self-assured.

Sometime around the age of 3, she impressed several observers with her independent nature. The children were being dressed in snowsuits in preparation for playtime in the snow. When I asked this three-foot-tall child to put on her mittens, she refused. No matter how much I threatened and cajoled, Giss held her ground. She absolutely would not put on the mittens. Rather than resort to force, I assumed she would come back for the damned mittens once her little fingers started to freeze. Outside she went. Another crises had been avoided and, surer than hell, she was soon at the door asking for the mittens.

She had difficulties as a student, probably because of dyslexia which was diagnosed in the first grade.

Besides, I think she was just plain bored with the whole school routine. Early in life, she would spend time working with Uncle Larry, with whom she bonded because of their mutual interests in carpentry, mechanics, and boating.

Giss is prone to correct whatever she considered to be an injustice. Sometimes this resulted in physical confrontation. There was one instance when her younger sister, Heather, *borrowed* Giss' ice skates without asking to use them. When Giss spied her sister skating with friends not far from our house, she lit into her, fists flying. Witnessing the ruckus, I immediately interceded, pulling the two girls apart. Heather heeded my actions and backed away, but not Giss. She turned on me in a rage. I noticed that her hair was actually rising on her scalp. The fists, which had been pounding Heather, were suddenly turned on me. I soon realized that Giss was out of control and took a different tactic. I turned on my heels and ran away. She chased me down the street! This was the only instance of physical confrontation with one of my children, and I came out of it unscathed and more conciliatory.

Like her older sister Jennifer, she had to be monitored carefully in her teen years. Amazingly, some of her friends, who exhibited dubious behavior while in high school, grew up to be fine people with successful occupations and families. Giss maintained some of these close friendships for decades.

After schooling, Giss was headed for the work world. She wouldn't be caught dead working in an office, and she would only wear a dress for special occasions. She preferred working in the out of doors whenever possible. One of her earlier jobs was as a service person for GE. She could attack any appliance with competence.

One time during football season, she was assigned to attend to an ailing GE refrigerator at a private home. At the time a group of five or six couples were glued to the TV watching a football playoff. When Giss arrived on the scene, complete with GE uniform and tool kit, the group was taken aback. They surely hadn't expected a female back in those days. A rousing cheer went up from the wives and girlfriends. Giss was their hero–a woman in charge!

Eventually she settled on the rural postal delivery service. She was assigned her own truck, was pretty much on her own, and she wasn't stuck in an office. And too, the pension and hospital benefits were generous.

As might be expected, Giss came home with some great stories garnered while driving the rural delivery route. One time, she was stopped at a mail box and noticed something peculiar perched on a passing van. It was a cat clinging to the ski rack on the roof of the van, holding on for dear life. Apparently the owner of the van had climbed into the vehicle and started on his way without noticing the cat sleeping on the roof.

Giss jumped into the mail truck and followed in hot pursuit. She rounded curves and picked up speed on the straightaway, all the time keeping an eye on the terrified cat atop the van. The cat kept looking back at the mail track and tenaciously kept its grip on the ski rack. Unfortunately, Giss could follow just so far and had to give up pursuit. She never found out what happened to the cat.

In another instance she was slowly passing a house on a hot summer day. Parked outside the house in the driveway was an SUV with the doors open. Two children were at play next to the car. What were they doing? Picking up garden snakes and putting them into the SUV! Giss couldn't let that continue so she abruptly stopped the mail truck.

"Do you kids realize what might happen when your mother is driving along and spies a live snake at her feet in the car?" Giss warned. "She could lose control of the car and have a terrible accident."

That must never have occurred to the children. Sheepishly they retrieved the snakes from the van and released them.

When it came to building a house, Giss was in her element, shoulder to shoulder with her husband, Steve, as together they did a major portion of the building process. Involvement in fitting siding, building a sturdy deck and painting took time and effort and the finished project was a fine-looking country home. The house is located on a few acres of land near my town house.

At the homestead, Giss' energy and skills have been invaluable. She can maneuver the backing up of a boat trailer with complete competence. Weed whacking, painting, equipment repair, tending to the compost toilet, managing boats, kayaking, training the dog–just name it and Giss will handle it. In addition to all of that, she continues to be a fine mother and a dependable employee.

She never lost her interest in partying and has had amazing experiences with family and friends on cruises, in Las Vegas, on traveling vacations, at the local night spot scene, and at home gatherings.

She has never flagged in her devotion to me–stopping by the house often and phoning to ensure that all is fine with me. Wow! Am I a lucky guy or what?

HEATHER

Daughter Heather was born in Melbourne, Australia. Sandy and I must have gotten carried away on our Hawaiian stopover on the way to my 1965-66 teaching assignment in the Land Down Under. We already had four youngsters.

We arrived in Melbourne in July, a chilly and wet time of the year. We knew no one initially, and the housing deal we had expected had fallen through. We took up temporary quarters, sharing the toilet and kitchen in a drafty, damp rooming house in the center of the city. I experienced a rare surge of sustained depression for a few days. Sandy never seemed to share my sagging spirits.

Three days of this depressing situation drove me to purchasing a newspaper and scanning the housing ads. I spotted a house rental in East Doncaster, in the suburbs far from the center of the city. The thoughtful rooming house landlord drove our family to our new home.

Our dwelling was for rent for a year because the owners were in the process of divorce. I paid a month's rent and a deposit and we *settled in* as the Aussies would say. The big advantage was that we had a comfortable home for our large family. There were several disadvantages, however. There was no indoor toilet although the owner had completed installing a shower and sink. There was no central heating. We had no radio or TV, nor did I have a vehicle. Getting to work in the center of the city involved a one-mile hike on a dirt road, boarding a bus and later transferring to a tram (trolley car). Regardless, the routine was much more acceptable that the dark and dank rooming house.

We had an elementary school nearby. Grocery shopping, however, was a physical challenge. At that point in time Melbourne had few super markets and so we got used to going to specialty shops: a green grocery for veggies and fruit, a milk bar for dairy products, a bakery for fresh bread, and a butcher shop for meat. It was fun to shop, even on our limited budget. The painful part was lugging the groceries home. But we managed.

Gradually as warmer weather approached, we had made some satisfactory adjustments. An American emigrant, Bud Johnson, let us borrow his paraffin (kerosene) heater, a significant albeit smelly improvement over the wood that had to be chopped, or the charcoal briquettes, which were expensive.

We also received a radio on loan from a teaching colleague. And, best of all, we made several Australian friends with whom I worked at the college.

And then there came an offer to buy a well-used Wolseley car from my boss, Allen Hulls, who became our closest friend while in Australia and for decades thereafter.

But I digress! This all leads to our realization that Sandy was once again pregnant. Offspring number five was due in March of 1966. She was named Heather Elizabeth. Her middle name with the double source from my sister, Elizabeth Jane, and also Allen Hulls' funloving wife.

Sandy went to a hospital not far from our home. It shocked me to learn that I was expected to be present in the delivery room. I had never done this with the other four children! I was downright terrified. I was even more terrified as I heard Sandy's screams. It didn't help to be clothed in a green gown let alone a face mask and cloth slippers. I wanted to bolt from the room and was very relieved when Sandy ordered me to leave. Soon after my departure, our healthy new dual-citizenship daughter came into the world–pink, ugly and squalling just like her older siblings.

My mother, upon receiving the news of the latest addition to my family, wrote "Yet another girl–ho hum." Obviously she favored male additions to the family.

When I arrived home after midnight, I could not sleep for the life of me. Here we were thousands of miles from home, earning a pittance, and striving to maintain a family of five children. How could I have done this to Sandy? What was going on in my head? I sank into deep anxiety and depression–for the rest of the night.

In the morning, reality set back in and my spirits soared. It was sunny and warm out. A neighbor had volunteered to babysit Jennifer and Kristina while I was at work. The boys would be in school. Everyone in the family were healthy. Elizabeth Hulls had given us three months of free diaper (nappy) service. The world looked rosier.

When we left Australia, another friend, Sally Clemens, had given us a basket in which to carry Heather. When we reached San Francisco, she was carried along with us to enjoy the cable cars and Chinatown, downtown and the wharf areas.

Heather has grown to be the most sociable of the offspring. Her spirits are uncannily high most of the times, somewhat reminiscent of my Aunt Bess and also brother Bleecker. Even when she contracted breast cancer and went through a double mastectomy, she was an inspiration to all.

In high school she was academically accomplished and also very popular as a cheer leader. And she made friends, friends, and more friends. Many of them were forgettable and several were of suspicious nature. I recall requesting her to bring her friends home so that we could get to know them. She did just as requested the following evening–23 of them lined up on the front porch seeking entertainment and refreshments! I never repeated the request.

And then there was the prom incident. Gaily Heather and several friends trooped off for a night of fun at the junior prom. "Don't make a ruckus coming home in the wee hours," I admonished her. "I don't want the neighbors signing a petition for us to move!"

At three a.m. I sleepily staggered to the window to find what the racket was all about. In the driver's seat of their rented limo, I spotted Heather at the wheel. The crumpled figure of the drunken hired driver was in the passenger seat. Somehow we avoided a petition.

There was a similar situation aboard the local cruise boat on the Hudson River. Heather besotted the captain, Hughey, and manned the steering wheel in his stead, wearing Hughey's captain hat and taking full charge. Most of the passengers were either friends or family, but I often wondered about those who just happened to pay the fare for a pleasant night on the river.

Afterward she attended Miss Austin's, a reputable Albany beauty school. Aunt Bess' memorable admonishment "don't let your wit run away with you" surely would have applied to the way Heather managed the graduation party put on by the beauty school. She and a few other colleagues thought it would be fun to surprise the school proprietor with a male stripper. The prim and proper Miss Austin was not at all amused!

Following beauty school, Heather and her two older sisters took an apartment along with a male cousin. Party time was the life style until the potential marriage partners arrived on the scene. Heather managed to find hers at a bar while visiting cousin Cheryl near Princeton, NJ. How she snagged this great find, I'll never know.

I'll never forget how Don Waters reacted to a remark I couldn't help directing to him upon his first visit to the family. I looked at him seriously and said, "I hope you haven't come all this distance without intending to marry my daughter!" His reaction, as expressed in his startled eyes, was abject fear. Little did I know that within a year he would propose.

As a matter of fact, Sandy and I had the *good fortune* of marrying off all three older daughters within the time span of one year. I think I'm still paying for the weddings. Steve Erby proposed to Giss; Don Waters presented a ring to Heather; and Craig Hoeffner married Jenn. In my opinion each of the husbands was a prize.

Heather and Don bought a house in New Jersey and became parents of three sons and a daughter. Heather remains the family spark, enlivening the homestead whenever she and her family visit. An invitation to surf or water ski behind a boat driven by Heather could result in broken bones.

Don and Heather have befriended five or six couples with whom they have kept contact for at least a score of years. It all started when Don and several buddies became soccer coaches for their children's teams. Since then some of the offspring have graduated from college, but still the parents see each other socially a few times a year.

GREG

Where he got the nickname "Siego" I'll never know but son Greg Arthur was tagged with that appellation for life. He was the sixth of our offspring and a wonderful change of pace after we'd had three girls in a row. He was always a loving son and particularly devoted to his mother.

Struggling with his sexuality in an era when it was not acceptable to be gay, Greg's grades in high school suffered and he had troubles finding social acceptance. Although he made many close friends in high school, he dropped out and later earned a GED through testing.

Greg gravitated toward the restaurant business in his late teens and became one of the top waiters at one of the region's most prestigious restaurants. Unfortunately, the life style of the late-hour establishment became more than Greg could resist. After the customers left, the staff would hang out at the bar and then later find an after-hours joint where they would enjoy liquid refreshments, smoking and other vices until daylight.

After several years, Greg took another serving job at TGIF, a chain restaurant across the USA. TGIF had a generous policy of allowing any employee to travel across the country, stopping along the way to earn some money at any of their eating establishments until they had enough to go on to the next TGIF of their choice. Greg took up on the offer and he and a lady friend earned their way from TGIF to TGIF until they wound up in Phoenix, AZ. There he found another popular oasis and stayed on for four years. By this time, his traveling companion had come back home to the Capital Region.

Eventually, Greg decided to return home. To assuage his mother's fears regarding cross country traveling, Greg told us that his friend, Loll, would fly out to Phoenix and that together they would rent a U-Haul trailer and tow it home with his possessions in the trailer. He didn't tell us that he had lost his driver's license while in Arizona. Knowing that he would share the driving with a trustworthy friend gave us peace of mind. He also guaranteed us that he would phone home every evening on the way back, sometimes letting Loll make the call.

We were deliberately shielded from the truth. It turned out that Loll, who had planned to fly out and drive home with Greg, had developed a serious back problem and couldn't leave the Albany area. We didn't know that our son had no driver's license nor did we know he was traveling solo.

As a cover-up, Greg would phone home from wherever he was staying for the night. The following evening Loll would phone, telling us how the trip was going. We didn't know that Loll was phoning from her home just a few miles from us.

It all unraveled once Greg was safely home. He then felt free to tell of us of the charade involving the phone calls. He also told us that he was stopped several times by state police and that he would immediately inform them that he had no driver's license. For some reason, the police were only interested in examining his U-haul for hidden drugs. Fortunately, Greg was clean.

Once back in the region, our son took an apartment and continued with his self-destructive life style. When his mother died from cancer, he disintegrated rapidly and eventually had to visit rehab facilities. He lost his job. Sister Jenn stepped in to make the necessary arrangements for rehab with local social services. She was able to clear up extremely high accumulated medical debts and unpaid taxes and get him into an AA program, and acquire Medicaid coverage for his medications.

For eight years after my wife passed away, Greg lived at home and helped out in so many ways. He would mow the lawn, shovel snow, vacuum, do laundry and prepare meals. I would try to make things as easy for him as possible by providing his housing costs and taking care of all of the bills. Arthritis set into my hips in 2010 and I became even more dependent on Greg's care.

While he was good company and a loving son, Greg continued to battle demons. Alcohol, smoking addiction and prescribed medications with conflicting reactions battled within his system for several years

In April of 2015, Greg was helping me out by filling a few gasoline containers to supply the homestead with fuel for lawn mowers and other equipment. He had complained of chest pains and had a supply of glycerin tablets. He had scheduled a stress test with his doctor. The gas containers were in the back of my pickup truck.

I kept track of his progress by watching the rear view mirror while sitting in the driver's seat. There were two fuel containers left to be unloaded when Greg was no longer visible through the rear view mirror. I stepped out of the truck and saw him lying on his back staring at the sky. Apparently he'd felt a heart attacking coming on and had laid down on his back in the grass. I phoned 911 and within a few minutes six medics arrived by ambulance, but Greg was gone. He was only 47 years old!

VICTORIA

The name Victoria Esther, the last of the seven offspring, sounded so regal to Sandy and I. Victoria is named after the second most populous state in Australia where we spent a most memorable year. Esther was my mom's name. In our usual family tradition of assigning nicknames, she was called "Frog" at an early age and it has stuck with her for all these decades.

There was a five-year gap between Vicky and her next older sibling, Greg, so we had yet another golden opportunity to spoil an offspring. She did very well in school, both academically and socially and was particularly adept at math. She took to it so well that she majored in it in college at SUNY Potsdam, NY. On a part-time basis she completed her Master's Degree.

All through her early and teen years, she was loving, focused and self-disciplined. Following college, Vicky taught math in Rensselaer secondary school for three years and then moved on to Mechanicville. She appreciated the fact that Mechanicville parents seemed more in control of their offspring than those in Rensselaer. Nevertheless, teaching teenagers has always been a challenge.

Vicky has exhibited two wonderful traits in her adult years. She is extremely thoughtful as well as competent. As an illustration of thoughtfulness, she has always been generous with her time and talent to her nieces and nephews, particularly the ones living in the local area. In the summertime, she will take them golfing; in winter they love it when she takes them to the slopes for either snowboarding or downhill skiing. When there are idle hours in the cooler months, she will start up parlor games which encourage fun and competition.

Competence and organization are Vicky's forte. Her computer capabilities are invaluable to me who is prone to encounter every type of pitfall imaginable. When the software acts up because of a virus, or because of something I have inadvertently done, she is there to solve the problem. If there is a technique with which I am unfamiliar, she is at hand to help me through the learning process. And she does all of this in good cheer and not in a scolding manner. If there is preparation needed for travel, Vicky is there to help with the packing and to ensure that no necessary items have been neglected. Often I am driven to exasperation over the details, but more often than not, I appreciate it when I look for something I'm sure was forgotten–and there it is–right where she stowed it.

When it comes to my medical attention, Vicky excels. She schedules appointments and makes it a point to meet me at the doctor's office whenever possible. She usually accompanies me into the examining room and, notepad in hand, jots down the highlights of the conversation. She asks questions and writes down the responses. After the session, she contacts her siblings using the internet and informs them of results, future appointments, etc. When it comes to medications (and I take several), she has developed a spreadsheet listing the types of medication and the schedule. Whenever we are requested to provide a detail of medications used, I simply produce the most recent computerized spreadsheet. The recipient is always pleased to receive such information in such organized fashion.

At home, I am continuously reminded to follow the medical regimen. It is posted near the area where I spend most of my time–and she checks on me to make sure I'm adhering to the schedule.

In recent years, Victoria has been interested in travel, particularly to Germany and Austria. For several years she has practiced learning the German language.

She has visited both countries not only to see the sights but to experience the culture—attending the opera, eating at sidewalk cafes and beer gardens, strolling in the parks. The visits have served to whet her appetite for even more.

In recent months, Vicky moved into the upstairs of my town house and she has become an excellent companion and caregiver. We respect each other's privacy and we share the bills. The entire family has consented to an agreement whereby after I pass on, the house will be left to all surviving offspring with the likelihood that Victoria will buy out her siblings.

My health problems accelerated in 2016. Vicky immediately stepped into the breach, and things have stabilized. Grace, blessings, love–I have abundance in all.

Grandchildren

Among the most precious rewards of the older years are grandchildren. Having produced the sizeable family of seven offspring, there was bound to be a generous quantity of them—15 including 3 terrific step-grandchildren brought into the family by Kathy's marriage to Grant.

MEGHAN—MARK'S DAUGHTER

Meg was the first of the crop. Fussing over our first grandchild was a wonderful experience. However, after Meg was two years old, we lost track of her because my son and her mother parted. It wasn't until her late teens that we have resumed a terrific relationship. Meg went to SUNY New Paltz and there majored in design. She was so talented in the designing area that she produced a teapot which she was able to sell some years later for thousands of dollars. Meg now lives in New Hope, PA, and works in a factory in a supervising capacity. In her spare time, she takes on-line courses and spends hours at physical fitness.

KEVIN—MARK'S SON

Mark's second child, Kevin, is now grown into manhood. As a teenager, he was one carefree dude, thoroughly enjoying his social life, and working two or three jobs to be able to afford it. He has chosen to go into construction work and now finds himself installing solar panels. It's outdoor work and he prefers it. He met and married an attorney, Rebekah, and they are the parents of two young children, Aurora and

Calvin. At present, they have decided to sample living in the south and have chosen the Raleigh, NC, area.

ETHAN—GRANT'S OLDER SON

Grant's offspring have remained a part of Sandy's and my lives in spite of their parents' divorce. Ethan has been a loving and active grandson. He determinedly works out to keep physically fit, particularly by setting up a regimen of running. He has developed a deep interest in entomology (insects) and has accordingly pursued a college career in that area. He has successfully earned grants with which to get hands-on experience in Costa Rica and in Ecuador. Snakes and lizards and frogs are his friends. Currently he is working toward his PhD at the University of Kentucky in Louisville, KY.

EVAN—GRANT'S YOUNGER SON

Evan is very dissimilar from his older brother. His interest when growing up was in the area of auto mechanics—and he is good at it! In his teens, he completely restored his Dad's 1969 Mustang. This involved separating the body from the frame and sanding down and painting both. Re-upholstery throughout. He even changed the automatic transmission to a stick shift drive which required major adjustment to the frame!

When I saw the results, I consented to let him restore my 1931 Model A Ford Roadster. He got right at it—taking out the engine, removing the radiator, taking off the headlights—and then he abruptly joined the Navy. Interestingly enough, he has found his way into the bomb handling area and seems to be thoroughly enjoying the training segment at the present time.

ZACHARY—JENN'S OLDER SON

Just writing about the grandchildren fills my heart with pride. Zach was unique from the outset. While still in a crib, he developed an intense love for apple juice. He drank so much that his teeth began to turn yellow. "More juice," he would demand, flinging his empty bottle out of the crib and against the wall. That behavior was forthwith corrected.

Zach, even in his early years, was inquisitive and his consistent question was. "Why?" driving us all to distraction.

He did extremely well academically all the way through public school. In his early teens, he gained extra weight—and assiduously worked it off by running to keep fit. When a teen ager, he developed a deep interest in orienteering—and it was his SEAL uncle Grant who got him involved. It has been Zach's interest throughout his adult life.

After graduating from secondary school, he was accepted at the Air Force Academy and graduated four years later. Following that, he has been stationed at Wright-Patterson air base in Dayton, OH. While there, he has taken on an offer to earn a Masters' Degree in both Applied Physics, and Nuclear Science.

NICHOLAS—JENN'S YOUNGER SON

When very young, Nicky was one cute little guy. Early on he developed a very keen interest in heavy-duty construction equipment—trucks, cranes, pay loaders, bulldozers, etc. It was very easy to find toys to suit him. For a while he was absolutely crazy about his John Deere toy collections, making beeping backup sounds and rumbling noises for going forward.

He has done well academically and, while in high school, Nick enjoyed skiing and golf, often accompanying Aunt Vicky to the slopes. He has also done considerable travel in his young years and has developed an interest in mountain climbing, hiking and exploration.

Following secondary school, he went to SUNY Stony Brook on Long Island, majoring in Biology. As this book is written, he is in Auckland, New Zealand, on an exchange student study program—and hiking and exploring while there.

MATTHEW—GISS' OLDEST SON

Matthew Erby, has, like the rest, been a great source of pride. His outgoing personality is a most endearing trait. Since his early years, Matt could walk into a room full of unfamiliar people and easily start a conversation with several of them. He was always well-behaved and very talented academically. In secondary school, he had several close friends with whom he has kept in touch.

I recall an example of Matt's humor when in secondary school. At the time, the older members of the family, including brothers Larry, Barry and I and a few friends, used to spend the late afternoon warm-weather hours at the homestead in an outbuilding called *The Oasis*. There we would while away the time sipping a beverage or more, chatting and enjoying each other's company. It never occurred to us that the younger generation was monitoring our fun.

Later on I learned that, when in their senior year in a careers class, the teacher had asked the students what they might like to do in later retirement life. Grandsons Ethan and Matthew, who both attended the class, cooked up a response. Others volunteered their options, for instance: moving to Florida–retiring to a posh assisted-living facility—sailing around the world. Matthew raised his and, when called upon said, "Ethan and I want to spend our time in the *Oasis*, drinking booze with our granduncles and my grandfather!"

After high school graduation, Matt went to the University of Rochester with a goal of becoming a medical doctor. He volunteered for EMT duty in his spare hours. Although accepted at both Harvard and Stanford Medical Schools, he chose SUNY Stony Brook, in order to save on taking out huge student loans. There he has had successful progress to date and is now sorting out his options for physician specialization.

BRANDON—GISS'S YOUNGER SON

Brandon was one of the cutest little kids imaginable. In his very young years, Sandy took care of both he and his cousin, Nicholas. They were really well behaved and fun to be around.

Once in a while, when Sandy had another commitment, I would take over as baby sitter.

When Brandon was 4 or 5, I taught him how to play cards—a game called WAR. It's a little hard to believe, but this sweet-looking kid taught himself how to cheat!

Brandon did well in public school and participated in rugby, football and soccer.

Following high school, he spent a year at the University of Alabama in Auburn, AL.

While visiting him there, I was amazed to see the huge football stadium which, I believe, held 70,000+ sports fans. After a year at Auburn, he transferred to Boston University and changed his major from biology to business.

TYLER—HEATHER'S OLDEST SON

Because they live in the Philadelphia area, frequent visits and electronic communications from the Don and Heather Waters family have kept us connected. Tyler was the first of their four children. When young, he was the image of his dad and had his mother's lively spirit. He has never been afraid of hard work—an admirable quality that has followed him into adulthood.

Tyler had a great time in high school, which he carried over when he went to the University of West Virginia at Morgantown. There he truly enjoyed four years of socializing. Although still a history buff, he is now back in his hometown working as a construction supervisor and union laborer. He enjoys work, lives independently and does a lot of reading. Along with all of that, he has become a physical fitness enthusiast, spending time at the gym and living a healthy lifestyle.

SAWYER—HEATHER'S SECOND SON

It was bound to happen that Sawyer's nickname would become "Saw". Much like his father, Sawyer is an avid sports fan, particularly fond of soccer. From an early age, Sawyer excelled at playing soccer and enjoyed taking charge of the field. Not one for incompetence, he makes a good leader—pushing his peers to compete at their very best.

Sawyer loves the warmth and beauty of Charleston, SC, where he has been enrolled at the Exercise Science degree at the College of Charleston, downtown in the city. He also spends his free time in the Reach program, helping disadvantaged children.

When he was in middle school, he pulled a stunt which surely showed resourcefulness. At about the middle of the fall semester of his senior year, Heather received a phone call from the high school guidance counselor's office: "Your son, Sawyer, has requested to drop choir and we don't allow students to drop a course in the middle of the term since he is obtaining credits for this course." Heather was confused and responded, "Drop choir—I didn't even know he was taking choir—have you ever heard him sing?" Let me get back to you after I've talked to him about this."

"Why are you taking choir? You never seemed interested in it."

"It's like this Mom," Sawyer confessed. "In late August when school started and the days were so hot and muggy, my buddy and I couldn't take the heat so we signed up for choir because the classes were held in the only air-conditioned room in the school. Now that the weather has cooled down, we don't need an air-conditioned classroom."

Ultimately, he adhered to the school policy and successfully completed the music course.

Sawyer thrives on a life of balance: studying hard, eating healthy foods, exercising and participating in sports. He is quiet with a fine sense of humor and a group of close friends.

CONNOR—HEATHER'S THIRD SON

Connor has been an exemplary grandson. He is quiet and polite, but readily joins into conversation when topics of interest encourage it. Throughout public school, he played sports, particularly soccer, and has showed academic talent.

He is now enrolled in a business program at the University of Pittsburgh and living in a fraternity dorm. College life is much to his liking. In his spare time, he works in a fast food eatery and in the summer, he works at a golf course.

To some, he seems just too good to be fun, but in recent years, I find that a bit of imbibing loosens him to become a thoroughly enjoyable conversationalist.

HANNAH—THE SECOND GRANDDAUGHTER

After having three sons in a row, Heather and Don Waters gladly welcomed the arrival of daughter Hannah. After nine males in a row, we were happy to see a second granddaughter arrive on the scene. She is a combination of her mother's inability to sit still and her dad's determination. Hannah has grown to be quite a young lady—strong willed with a mind of her own. She has a knack, through conviction, for getting want she wants.

During her high school years, Hannah baked and sold cupcakes for which she raised over two thousand dollars to finance a People to People tour of Australia,

Fiji, and New Zealand. She later started at a state college in Indiana, PA, but found it to be too remote and thence transferred to Long Island University (LIU) in Brooklyn where she is pursuing a nursing career. In addition to carrying a full time class load, she carries two jobs and has recently purchased a car of her own.

Hannah can be most helpful, not only by taking on chores herself, but by persuading her cousins to pitch in with needed work at the homestead.

Grandchildren through Remarriage
Dan Kirsch

Somehow I like to steer clear of using the term "step-grandchildren"— it makes me think of those Grimm's fairy tales where "step" connoted wickedness or cruelty. Treating Grant's additional sons acquired through Kathy as my own grandchildren seems such a better way to handle the situation. Since her three boys didn't become part of my family until adulthood, I can only make judgements about them in recent years.

Dan, the eldest has always been interested in political science and has earned a PhD in that field. Currently he is teaching in a military secondary school in Pennsylvania and is married to a Unitarian Minister, Morgan McLean. Conversations with them both are interesting and stimulating.

TJ Kirsch

"TJ" is a soft-spoken guy who is extremely competent in his profession as a cartoon artist. He works out of his home. He and his wife, Crissy, have recently become parents, delighting his mother, Kathy, in her new career as a grandmother and part-time babysitter.

Alex Kirsch

In secondary school, Alex played in a band with close friends as so often teenagers do. He went away to college in Tennessee and became interested in a Hindu-related religion. At present, he is fulfilling his life's mission with fellow monks in the southern sector of India.

Great Grandchildren

Sometime along life's path, just about everyone contemplates at what age they might pass on. When in my twenties, I was sure I would die in my 50s since that was my father's age—but he had died accidentally. In my 40s I revised my life expectancy to my 70s since my uncles were making it that far before dying of natural causes. It never occurred to me that I would make into my 80s! There are some terrific *perks* that come with advanced years—grandchildren and great grandchildren.

There isn't too much to say about very young children. To me, they all seem to resemble Winston

143

Churchill when they are born. Their dispositions vary with their level of comfort and happiness—cranky to cheery. I prefer them cheery. In order of age, my great-grandchildren are (1) Aurora, daughter of grandson Kevin and his wife, Rebekah (2) Calvin, by the same parents as Aurora, and (3) Charlie, a daughter born to TJ Kirsch and his wife, Crissy.

At this stage of my life, I thoroughly enjoy being in on conversations with my children and grandchildren since they have all become mature and have developed their own distinct personalities. The great grandchildren are fun to hear about and to hold, and I'm sure they'll be more enjoyable company in later years.

Four

Physical Setbacks

My alarmed negative reaction to reaching age 83 is probably related to the health situation as well as to other factors. In general, my family was relatively free of chronic health problems. Minor ailments such as tonsillitis, appendicitis, chicken pox, and measles passed through the family without causing serious setbacks

Previously, the earlier generations had died from heart complications, particularly congestive heart failure. That cause of demise diminished during the 1950s and '60s because of amazing progress in treating heart problems. While it was common for my predecessors to die in their 60s or 70s from heart problems, exercise, better eating habits, bypass surgery, etc. significantly cut down heart-related death. Now cancer seems to have taken over, but we are living into our 80s, some 20 years beyond previous generations.

JAUNDICE

I had a serious bout with jaundice at age 5. Interestingly, it emanated from our vegetable garden, where the handyman from next door had used outhouse waste for fertilizer. Although my coloring changed to a pale yellow and I was hospitalized for a few days, I recovered rapidly. The only lasting effect was that I have never been able to donate blood because the jaundice remains in my bloodstream.

THE BURNING ACCIDENT

A nearly fatal accident came about on an early November day in 1939. My brothers and I had built an outdoor fire a few hundred feet from the house. I was sitting with my back to the fire when the wind changed direction and, unnoticed by me, caught my sweatshirt afire. When the realization came, it was too late. Flames were shooting out from under my sweatshirt.

Frantically I bolted toward the river, hoping to put the fire out by diving into the water. Fortunately one my brothers tackled me and he and others rolled me over and over, snuffing out the flames.

The burns damaged my legs, underarms, neck and a small patch on my skull. Wrapped in a blanket, I was loaded into the car of neighbor Mike Podoba and was taken to Albany City Hospital, now known as Albany Medical Center.

The prevailing burn treatment at the time was something called gentian violet which was a liquid healing medication spread over the scarred area.

Although more than 70 years ago, I clearly remember so much of the hospital stay. I was a patient on the sixth floor for four full months. Visiting hours were restricted to only Wednesday and Saturday afternoons, and my mother missed only one or two due to other obligations. My third grade teacher, Florence Holmes, came faithfully every Wednesday.

Late in my stay, I recall someone bringing in a battery-operated radio for my use.

Thereafter, I stayed glued to afternoon serials which included Dick Tracy, the Lone Ranger and Hop Harrigan–Ace of the Airways. I also recall being scared out of my wits once in the early hours of the morning when I opened the door of my hospital bedroom cabinet and witnessed a flood of cockroaches spill out over the floor and onto my bedding!

Nursing care was plentiful and indulgent. I discovered that I liked the taste of the filtered out pineapple juice after the pulp had settled to the bottom of the jar. I frequently asked for it and it came whenever requested. The nurses fawned over me. One who was particularly attentive, Peg Summerville, left hospital nursing to serve in the army. Her ship was torpedoed by a German submarine and all passengers went missing in action. Another loving attendant was someone named Catherine Stevens. I so often wonder whatever happened to her.

The doctors came and went and I don't recall most of them, with the exception of Dr. Harold Browne. Was it not for him, I would have been disabled for life, with a left arm webbed tightly to my side, and my chin webbed to my chest. The scars were that bad!

The time was the late 1930's and plastic surgery was in its infancy. Dr. Browne, who was in his early 40's, took an interest in that field. At the time, there was little in the line of experience. He asked my mother if she would be willing to let me be his guinea pig as his first plastic surgery patient–at no cost!! My mother eagerly consented. No one wanted me to go through life so obviously disfigured.

My first hospital stay lasted through March of 1940. I spent some time at home and had to repeat the third grade since I'd only attended that level for two months prior to the accident.

There were to be five skin graft operations, each occurring in the summer so that I wouldn't miss school.

How I hated giving up part of the summers to go into the hospital. Dr. Browne would take skin from the front of my upper leg and piece it onto the scar tissue, both on my neck and under my left arm. He would slice the scar tissue and insert grafted skin to form more attractive facial features.

These operations were spread over several years. Strange that I can so clearly remember things that occurred several decades ago. I recall the Doctor's office smelling aromatically of cigar smoke. He liked big stogies, and for some time in my 20s and 30s I thoroughly enjoyed them as well. I also remember that he had a pure-bred curly-haired button-eyed Airedale Terrier dog named Susie which befriended his patients in the waiting room.

HEART SURGERY

In my late 60s I had two or three physically distressing sensations during which my lower right side jaw would ache for several minutes and then the pain would subside. It happened once while singing in the choir and on a later occasion while riding in an outboard motor boat on the Hudson River. It was worrisome and I consulted with a good friend who was the receptionist for a woman who was to become my cardiologist for more than 20 years.

Dr. Jana Hoffmeister used her expertise in diagnosing my heart problem and recommending treatment. I was scheduled for a catheterization. For me, the catheterization was a fascinating experience. Amazing to see a foreign probe snaking its way through my arteries!

A few days later, a double bypass was performed by a young specialist who used a new procedure: operating by opening my ribs in the upper chest rather than the traditional method of breaking through the sternum. I guess it would not have worked if more remote arteries were endangered.

All seemed to go very well as far as the healing process was involved until several weeks later when I seemed to lose strength and became listless. I'm told that I turned grey! Surer than hell, I was allergic to a drug, Ticlid, which had been prescribed for me and which has since been taken off the market. It was sapping my red blood cells near to the point of fatality. Once that problem was solved, my heart attacks never reoccurred.

Dr. Hoffmeister and I became fast friends. She had a wonderful sense of humor, but she took no nonsense.

There was the Lipitor incident. After taking the drug for several months, I began having painful leg cramps during the night. A friend and self-styled shaman had the answer: "Stop taking Lipitor. Take Niacin instead–it's just as good for you and you won't get the cramps." At my next visit to Dr. Hoffmeister, she exclaimed, "What has happened to your cholesterol count. It's dangerously sky high!"

"I'm substituting Niacin for Lipitor because I can't deal with the leg cramps which give me nighttime pain.

She furrowed her eyebrows and snarled back at me, "Go back to the Lipitor. You will take the pain!" I think of her when the leg cramps recur.

URINARY DISTRESS

The decade of my 60s ushered in several serious problems and also minor setbacks.

Fortunately these problems weren't debilitating. Cumulatively speaking, however, they are a pain the butt. The diabetes and blood pressure problems came with overweight which has plagued me throughout life. I eat too much of the wrong things. In recent years, bladder distress has also become a most annoying irritant. It seems that my bladder requires emptying every hour or so, even during the night.

Coping with this recurring annoyance has become routine. I carry an empty coffee container in the front seat of the car because the walk to a filling station lavatory or a rest stop men's room becomes a painful journey exacerbated by hip arthritis. My tactic is to make wise use of interstate rest stops–taking the truck entrance and parking obscurely next to an unoccupied behemoth of a semi provides the anonymity of privacy to relieve myself.

Making light of the situation helps. I tell my young friends that there are definite benefits to growing old.

"Do you know how relieved you feel when you finally are able to pee after holding it for hours? Well, I have that sensation of relief about twelve times a day!"

ARTHRITIS

The onset date of my arthritis is clearly etched in my mind. It was in the winter of 2010 and I was 78. I decided to make one last trip to Australia to visit my 1960s colleagues there. If I had put it off just one more year, my closest friend would not have been able to spend time with me, because in the next year, 2011, he was in a rehab center following a crippling stroke.

Aussies love to boast about their physical fitness. They walk everywhere it seems. I'd be damned if I would lag behind putting with up with such jibes as "You Yanks are soft."

One time my friends decided on a lunch time meeting at an out-of-the-way eatery in Melbourne. Suspecting a challenging walk, I asked my good friend, Allen, "How far will it be from the parking area to the restaurant?" "Just a few steps," he curtly replied.

Those "few steps" amounted to a trek of several city blocks which had me damned near dropping in my tracks. Not only did I have to make it to the eatery, but I also had to make the return trip. The experience was painful, particularly in my hips. The longer I stayed in Melbourne, the more walking I did and I found myself searching out benches when walking with a friend and his dog in the park.

When I got home, I immediately made an appointment with a bone specialist. Something had changed and the pain didn't seem to be easing as time passed.

My initial appointment was with a woman orthopedist whose specialty was the spinal column. Her bedside manner left a lot to be desired. Upon examining my tests, she authoritatively commented, "Do you have any idea how poor your health is?" Actually, I didn't. With the exception of aching joints, I felt fine. She, however was examining records which revealed high blood pressure, type 2 diabetes, borderline kidney problems–all that in addition to my back problems.

She referred me to another bone specialists who specialized in hip disorders. Daughter Vicky, who had become a saint in terms of shepherding me to various doctor appointments, Googled this new contact and found him to be an internationally reputed expert who'd given lectures around the world.

The doctor was in his 60s. His diagnosis and recommendations were brief. "You have arthritis in your hips and soon will have it in your knees," he said. "I'm sure it is very painful. However, I recommend that you *do not* have surgery or even resort to an injection of any kind. The reason is that you have other health problems such as diabetes and high blood pressure and that doing anything about it, other than taking pain relievers, could result in your being in bed and/or wheelchair for the rest of your life!"

That was certainly hard-to-swallow advice and so the discomfort when walking has become a way of life. After about 20 steps, I have to pause and rest. It just plain hurts to walk. In a way, though, there are compensations. I still can sleep in total comfort and driving the car presents no problem at all. And I can enjoy a good swim, thank heaven.

There was one memorable incident at the hip specialists' office. He asked Vicky, dressed in shorts and looking chic, to help him demonstrate how my leg action *should* work. He asked her to lie down on the patient's bed and then he proceeded to gently grasp her right leg below the knee. He worked her leg up and down, indicating how the process of proper walking should work–as opposed to the limp I had exhibited. It somehow seemed strangely kinky to have him holding my daughter's bare leg in his hands.

When we got outside the office, both of us had a good laugh trying to decide whether the doctor was using professional judgement or whether he was just another dirty old man.

OTHER PHYSICAL HEALTH PROBLEMS

Declining health has be expected when the 80s set in. For one, eye problems, particularly cataracts. An operation on the right eye has been necessary but other than that I have been wearing glasses for reading ever since my mid-20s.

Hearing? Ask my offspring because my deafness drives them bananas. It has become increasingly worse since I reached my 60s. In the past year, I broke down and bought hearing aids just to shut them up. I find them to be of very little use. I can hear the minister and the choir more clearly. Most voices, particularly raspy ones, are no problem. But a muffled low voice remains relatively inaudible. Those genteel British ladies speaking in *Downton Abbey* with their soft voices are most challenging. I find *Close Captioning* on the TV to be much more helpful in that situation.

Skin cracking problems relate back to when I was severely burned and hospitalized at the age of seven, followed by skin-grafting operations. I have learned that scar tissue can present problems in advanced age. In very recent years, lesions have appeared on sun-drenched areas. Some have benign cancer and require expert attention. The possibility of deadly melanoma is not to be ignored.

MENTAL STATUS

Fortunately, (at least in my humble opinion) there have no problems with mental health to date. I have had the normal mood swings and was inclined toward temper tantrums in my early years. I have had mild experiences with depression. In recent times, I have found myself worrying about things over which I have no control such as frustration at not being able to perform physical activities–walking, carpentry, travel, home chores, etc. As I understand it, such frustrations are very common for the elderly.

I have been blessed to find humor in just about every aspect of life. I treasure good stories and jokes and reading materials. Having fun friends, work associates and family over the years has been a source of joy.

It's much healthier to be optimistic. Now and then I'll come upon someone who thinks the world is going to hell in a handbasket and I couldn't disagree more. While the international news of conflicts is often discouraging, I somehow feel that things will turn out right. I think my family and friends and spirituality provide the fortification for positive thinking. When I listen in on my maturing grandchildren's conversations, I remain optimistic about the future.

I lament the decline of main-line church attendance by many of today's youth, but am convinced that they maintain wholesome morals and have simply been turned off by organized religion.

Strong family ties have been a source of strength over the decades. For as long as I can remember, Sunday dinners with extended family have taken place at the homestead. When I describe these weekly gatherings to friends, they often express admiration and envy.

Five

SOCIAL LIFE

Being brought up in a large, gregarious family has been a blessing which has been a major influence on my life. Although there have been some occasional breaches, we have somehow focused on getting along and really enjoy each other's company.

Early years

Our family had an enviable combination of both country and city living, and–because most of my siblings and I were extremely outgoing–continuous enjoyable relationships were an integral part of daily life. In the city there was a steady flow of friends even though we were restricted by the sleeping schedule of my railroad-engineer uncle. Nevertheless, the house was usually bustling, particularly in my teen years and beyond.

At the homestead, the arrivals and departures at the parking lot seemed endless. We enjoyed it that way. People came on foot, bicycle, by hitchhiking, bus and, of course, automobile. The walk between Rensselaer and the homestead was just about five miles, and those who very occasionally used that mode of transportation used a dirt road which wandered through the corn fields and sand flats along the river.

I clearly recall the day when two of my young country neighbors and I chose to walk barefooted to the city just for something to do on a steamy summer afternoon. We weren't more than five or six years old at the time. When we arrived in Rensselaer, we were hot and tired and desperately in need of a drink of water. It was my expectation that Aunt Bess would be delighted to see us. NOT!

The lady was very upset upon having three dirty shoeless urchins on the doorstep. She scolded us for *risking our lives* on a hot summer day. I'll never know why. After all, there was no traffic on the quiet obscure dirt road and predators were totally beyond our comprehension. Well, we got a good scolding and then a drink of water, and then a drive back to the country by a neighbor who shared Aunt Bess' fears.

In later years, most of us had bicycles or hitch-hiked using our thumb. When biking, we generally chose the *back* road, the dirt road close to the river. Although more challenging than the paved Route 9J, there was less traffic. Barry's friend, Wil Koveleskie, once volunteered to pedal his bike carrying both brother Bleeck and I as passengers. I rode on the handlebars and my brother straddled the brace over the rear wheel. It became an eventful ride when darkness set in and a skunk wandered much too close for comfort. In addition there were the usual challenges of ruts, puddles and those stray rocks that poked up through the dirt road in oh-so-many places.

Hitchhiking, to us, became an art form. In those days, there was little threat of predators, drunks or druggies manning vehicles. The chances of being picked up was a slender one but worth the try. One or two hiking together was the usual arrangement. If it was felt that two were one too many, there was the ploy of having only one hiker alongside the highway with his buddy hiding on the roadside ditch. The car operator would stop and offer a lift, and the hiker would innocently inquire if there was room for just one more passenger. If agreeable to the driver, the companion would bound out of his seclusion. I say *his* because girls were never encouraged to hitchhike.

On one daring occasion, there were three of us hitching along route 9J. We decided that three together was overwhelming, so we split into three singles about one quarter of a mile between us. My brother got the first ride. When the second one was sighted, he asked the driver if he would mind picking up his friend. Hesitatingly, the driver consented.

With the two ensconced in the vehicle, number three appeared another stretch down the road. Imagine the nerve of asking the driver to extend his hospitality to one more passenger!

"Could you please stop and pick up my other friend?" my brother inquired. "What do you think: that I'm running a taxi service?" the driver snarled. Hiker number three was out of luck and had to walk the entire five miles.

There was always something to do at the homestead, and in our teen years, the freedom from parental control was an added benefit.

There was little money among us, so we would make do with a slice of bread covered with mustard and sprinkled with sugar. Sounds awful but it seemed to hit the spot. We did a lot of billiard playing in the colder months along with outdoor activities including

sledding, ice skating and tobogganing. The knoll behind the house wasn't high enough for skiing.

To keep warm, we fed sawed-up railroad ties into wood
stove lengths for the kitchen, living room, and upstairs
bedroom. It never occurred to us that the creosote in railroad ties caused soot which would block the chimneys.
When the stove smoked, we let the fire go out and took
down the stovepipe and knocked out the soot by beating
the pipe against the stone wall around the gardens.

As we grew into our teen years, my mother would
trust us to bring along buddies to share the fun at the
homestead. Most of sister Janey's friends were summer
companions who spent winters in the city.

Larry's buddies would travel to the homestead by
bike and sometimes when Larry borrowed the Model
A Ford from my mother. Larry was a great mechanic
and kept the car in running condition. He also used
it as a gag prop, sometimes carrying a dummy in the
rumble seat or maybe just a dummy's leg protruding
from the closed rumble seat. A favorite trick of his was
to rev up the engine, turn off the key, and then turn
the key back on. An ear-splitting explosion would en-
sue, which would scare any nearby unsuspecting by-
stander into shock. This prank would often result in
the muffler splitting up the middle, rendering it useless for controlling engine sound–but, what the hell, a
replacement muffler was a whopping $15.

Brother Kim's teenage buddies were more interested in hunting and camping. For an investment of $20, Kim acquired an ugly, well-worn lifeboat once used by the river cruise line. Creatively, he installed a cabin and a well in the rear for affixing an outboard motor. There would usually be one or two overnight camping trips a summer along the Hudson going southward to take advantage of empty beaches on the east side of the river. Kim and a few friends would stock in provisions and cruise away for a few days. Their leisure was spent swimming and beach exploring. Driftwood along the shore was in significant abundance for an impromptu fire.

Brother Bleeck and I would watch with anticipation as Kim prepared for a camping trip, hoping that we would be asked to join in the adventure. Unfortunately, we were too young to make the cut. "Should we take the little shits?" was a question which invariably came up, Bleeck and I wished with all our hearts to be selected, but the decision would be a resounding "NO." and "They'd be too much of a pain in the ass." Actually, Bleeck was more anxious to go than I. My reason: I hated the taste of canned evaporated milk which was the sole source of liquid refreshment. Even today, I look with disgust of the label "Carnation Evaporated Milk" on the cans which are still sold in super markets.

Barry's friends were a fun-loving group. They, too, enjoyed the Model A, taking it to high school basketball games. One frigid February night, Barry and his friend George Benkly drove off to attend a game in Castleton. Driving the car, a canvas-topped roadster with ineffective side curtains and a totally inadequate exhaust manifold heater, was a daunting experience. On the way home after the game, the radiator overheated. It was night and their recourse was to stop at a frozen-over stream near the homestead. To get to the water, Barry had to chop through the ice with an axe. Needless to say, the experience was a nightmare, the description of which was repeated over the ensuing decades.

Strip poker was a unique form of entertainment. Our variation was the same as regular draw poker with the additional requirement that a player who lost a hand would take off an article of clothing. The game was over when the biggest loser was stark naked. Of course there is always someone who thinks up a way to beat the system. In that group, it was friend Wil Koveleskie, who was a cheater par excellence. Wil would simply dress in multiple layers of clothing. In spite of losing several successive hands at poker, Wil always had enough shirts and pants on to avoid the humiliation of winding up naked.

Wil was an inveterate cheat. Even when he and Barry played a card game to pass the time, Barry had to be on the alert. One time he seated Barry in a chair behind which was a mirrored bureau. Another time, Wil had cleverly punched a hole in the corner of a card. To make matters worse, he was proud of his *talent!*

Brother Bleeck's teen buddies seemed to enjoy the pool table and billiards more than anything else. My teen groups were mainly composed of jocks who spent their time in sports activities. When we went to the island, it seems we spent the evening hours sitting in the living room and talking about the attractive chicks at school.

One of my high school buddies had his own club house in his back yard. Some eight or ten of us would gather at the club house on Saturday mornings. We would sit around the woodstove listening to the weekly tally of top hit tunes posted in *Billboard* magazine. That was heaven for me, because I was a rabid fan of the Andrews Sisters, and they were invariably on the list of top selling phonograph records in the late '40s and early '50s.

Alcohol was seldom a factor in any of these teen age get-togethers. My mother had no tolerance for any type of titillating beverage, and we adhered to her rules.

I do recall the mother of my buddy with the club house making intermittent appearances with the offer of cookies and milk, but I suspect she was simply monitoring our behavior when girls were in our midst.

My four eldest brothers all served in World War II, therefor social life was very limited during the war years. When the war ended and all were home from the service, all hell broke loose. Brother Kim was not involved because he had married and left the nest. Brothers Larry and Barry, however, lived at home for a few years and their action-filled social life was awesome.

Brother Bleeck had joined the Navy. I was too young at 15 to partake in the many social events which by this time included bar hopping by brothers Larry and Barry.

Square dancing was popular. It was a wholesome physical activity often offered at places that did not serve alcohol.

In 1950 I reached age 18 and joined in on the night life. I can recall going to a high school senior prom with the girl of my dreams, who just didn't happen to share my infatuation. At any rate, after the prom a few couples made the daring decision to spend time at a nightclub on the outskirts of Albany which offered purely adult entertainment. My date was a subdued, ladylike companion who should never have been taken to such a place. Another girl in the group had been born deaf.

The entertainment was a local comic who had a lewd but not over-the-top show. He had a lot of visually naughty displays such as a velvet 2" thick and 8" long dark colored rope dangling from his fly. His jokes were off color but not filthy. Nevertheless, the one person among us who was totally hearing impaired, was so offended that she arose and demanded to be taken home. That broke up our party. It struck me funny that even though this girl couldn't hear the dirty jokes, she had sense enough to see that the show was inappropriate.

Some years later, I took this same girl of my dreams out canoeing on the Hudson River. I guess I never knew how naïve she was, even though at the time she was a sophomore in college. The Hudson can get polluted and there are the ubiquitous used condoms afloat. My date, upon seeing a few of these white rubber tubes commented: "look at all those balloons floating by—there must be a lot of parties going on." I had to stifle my laughter and was amazed that in her early 20s she had no idea what a condom looked like. It took me a few dates later to give her the straight scoop. After a few beers one evening I finally got up the courage. "Helen," I said, "I need to talk to you about those balloons you saw when we were canoeing on the river a few weeks ago." Boy, was she embarrassed not to have known about condoms. Decades later, after we had gone our own ways and had grown families, we still get together socially and invariably, the condom incident comes up.

Romances with college girls were few and far between. I found another girl of my dreams who consented to attend a formal with me. I was starry-eyed and overwhelmed, but perhaps it was my leering at her generously-sized bosoms that scared her off. Anyway she was beautiful and personable and worth the heart palpitations.

Another prom partner was a girl who, I think, was convinced she looked like Elizabeth Taylor, the Hollywood raving beauty at the time. Liz Taylor she was not. She wasn't at all pleased when I showed up in my Model A Roadster to take her to a prom. She was wearing a white hoop skirt gown and it had to be stuffed into the cramped front seat. Nor did I make any points when a few streaks of grease found their way onto her flowing gown. But she was a nice one-time date. As mentioned at the book's beginning, the 20s were frustrating years for me.

In 1950 a friend introduced me to her friend, Evie, and we struck it off so well that it developed into a more lasting relationship. She was short with a dazzling smile and a fun personality. Our mutual sense of humor was somewhat jaded. Of all things we both enjoyed hearing people *pass gas*. For two years, I didn't have to worry about getting a date–this girl was the right one for me.

It could have developed into marriage but religion became an insurmountable stumbling block. She was a devout Roman Catholic and I adhered to my Calvinistic Dutch Reformed background with tenacity. In those days, the Catholics had rigid rules about vowing in writing to bring up children in the *True Faith,* and a number of prohibitions that to me were unacceptable. For instance, my loved one could not attend a Protestant worship service. Evie did just that and was afraid throughout the service that she might be stricken by lightning or be seen by someone from her own church.

While it lasted, however, our relationship was fun. Eventually, fate stepped in and solved our problem. The Korean War came about and we guys in our 20s were required to do at least two years of active military service. I chose the Navy. It was less dangerous and the food was better than in the Army. Besides, four of my brothers were sailors.

I remember the decision to enlist when I did. My closest buddy literally talked me into it on an October evening in 1952. I was in college but bored with formal education after 14 straight years of it. "We'll enlist together and go to boot camp. It'll be so much fun," he reasoned. It didn't take much persuasion. On a bitter December morning, I stood at the railroad station awaiting the train to whisk me off to boot camp and two years of activity duty in the Navy. I stood there alone–my closest friend had met the lady of his dreams a few weeks earlier, and his plans to enlist melted away.

Going into the Navy answered the dilemma of about whether or not to get engaged. Within three weeks, Evie dumped me for a guy she'd met at work. I was heartbroken but, in time, relieved. The faith issue would never have been resolved.

Over the years, those religious differences have considerably evaporated. Tolerance has been a blessing and bigotry recognized for all its devastating consequences. For me, attitudes of intolerance toward religion, races, and sexual orientation preference have ebbed, and it has made my world one hell of a lot more enjoyable. I have found that, once one gets to know people in a minority group, one becomes much more accepting because it doesn't take that long to find out how much alike we all are in terms of outlook, family life, psychological problems. etc.

The Military

Or family heritage has been affected by members who were active in the military, including me. Early in the book, Colonel Phillip Staats, an American Revolutionary War hero, was mentioned. I'm sure that there have been family members in the military throughout the eleven generations. My first personal contact was with Uncle Allen who served in the Army in the Great War.

World War II prompted the enlistment of my three eldest brother, all in the Navy. Brother Kim saw considerable action aboard the submarine *USS Whale*. Brother Larry went to the Philippines but didn't became involved in any military action. Brother Barry made it as far as Texas. After the war ended, brother Bleecker enlisted in the Navy and then later joined the Coast Guard.

I went on active duty from the Naval Reserve during the Korean War but saw no military action. The Navy sent me to tropical Puerto Rico one summer and then to frigid Newfoundland the following winter.

I have fond memories of the service, particularly the friends encountered from all over the country. In boot camp. I teamed up with a guy from North Carolina who later became our NCO. Our friendship lasted long after Navy days, until he passed away in West Virginia at age 78. Following the military service, he'd attended divinity school and become a pastor and was instrumental in starting a senior assisted-living home in Huntington.

Following boot camp came Quartermaster school. When at the ship's helm, I looked like the Gorton's Fisherman guy. Made it to quartermaster 3rd class.

AGING SUDDENLY AT 83 (On the Hudson)

My first assignment was aboard the sea-going tug, USS *Allegheny*, moored at Floyd Bennett Field in Brooklyn. I can never forget the challenge of getting to the ship. I had left the subway terminal in Brooklyn at about midnight toting a very heavy canvas sea bag which contained all of my clothing. No taxis or buses were in sight, and I had no luck at all in sticking out my thumb. Eventually, I resigned myself to carrying the heavy bag on my shoulder for the three mile walk along Flatbush Avenue toward my destination. It was extremely hot and muggy that summer night as I trudged toward the Navy pier at the air field.

Eventually, carrying the bag became a burden I could no longer endure, so I dragged it behind me instead–block after city block. My spirits were down and my senses dulled, but eventually I came to realize that for some reason my load was becoming lighter. That's when I stopped and looked back. Talk about discouragement! Behind me I saw a trail of clothing: uniform tops and bottoms, shorts, t-shirts, socks, etc.! Dragging the bag caused the canvas to fray and eventually tear open, gradually spilling the contents along the street. So I gathered up it all and somehow struggled the rest of the distance to my destination.

For me, seasickness was a constant source of anguish. Every time the last rope was untied and we put to sea, my stomach began to heave. It was awful because there was no way to avoid the pitches and endless rolling that are peculiar to a relatively small vessel. Why eat? It only came back up. In fact it came back up so often that I had a chance to analyze the process. One time I kept track of the order in which I ate the food: first the beans, then the potatoes, then the meat, then the dessert. Sure enough, just as I suspected, it heaved out in the reverse order: first the dessert, then the meat, then the potatoes, etc. I guess I thought it would come out all blended together but maybe not so close in time to having the meal. Imagine making a study out of seasickness! On later occasions as I was hanging over the railing, I agonizingly said to myself, "Well, there go the beets. Next it will be the rice."

On one of the ships our electrician's mate had a sardonic time making fun of those of us who got seasick. He just thought that was the funniest thing and laughed as we suffered. Well, once off the coast of Nova Scotia we had a beauty of a storm and that tug pitched and rolled worse than ever. I crawled up to the window of the radio shack and heard this ugly continuous volley of retching. I looked into the porthole, and there was the radio guy heaving his guts out into a trash can. I couldn't help but yell, "that's the way, friend. Keep it up. You're doing a fine job!" He was green!

Once I thought I would try to avoid the sickness by counter action. Before leaving home and going out to sea I slugged down a whole bottle of wine, thinking a good buzz would offset the seasickness. Boy, was

I wrong! Combining a hangover with seasickness just doubled the agony.

The *Allegheny* had a total crew of about 25 so we all got to know each other in just a few weeks. Because the captain was a despot, somewhat like Captain Queig, the underlings' relationships jelled. I recall an instance when the cook, a friendly good-humored African-American, served us spaghetti and meatballs, but made the unpardonable error of forgetting to serve the captain. He had thrown the leftovers into the garbage can. Soon a voice in the intercom boomed, "Cook! Where is my dinner?" George cheerily responded, "Coming up, Captain," whereupon he selected a plate, took the lid off the garbage can, reached in with his hands and picked up enough spaghetti to fill the plate. Then he selected a few meatballs and placed then decoratively on top of the dinner plate. Who would know the difference? We all thought too much of George to tell his secret. He probably could have been court martialed.

For the second time in my Navy career, I made a friend–a coal miner from Pennsylvania who, after the service, earned a mining degree and rose to manage a huge Bethlehem Steel site near Johnstown, PA. As time passed we kept in contact and had a lot of time together. We each had several children. To this day, we visit each other even though impaired hearing and other physical limitations have set in.

The sea-going tug found its way to Puerto Rico and there my life was further enriched. Did I take advantage of an invitation by a buddy to bicycle and take a photo tour of the island? Oh no. Rum-and-coke concoctions were an overpowering magnet, and like so many of the crew, I spent hours at bars near the Navy base.

It was my first introduction to the shady side of life when I was introduced to swarms of prostitutes. Thank God, good old Aunt Bess had inculcated me with an abiding fear of social diseases. The *ladies of the night* seemed to flood into San Juan in hourly waves beginning early in the evening. Their pricing policy was unique, a study in combinations and permutations. The cost of an encounter was always quoted in three segments: the taxi, the room, and the girl herself. It could be "one for me, two for the room and two for the taxi," or "one for the taxi, one for the room and three for me," or even "two for me, three for the room and none for the taxi." But it always added up to $5 on the nose

A few shipmates contacted gonorrhea and other got something called *the clap*. One had something referred to as *crabs* which were lice-like highly contagious genital parasites. His last name was Rudford and he was from the hill country of Kentucky. A nice kid but in need of some guidance. For contacting the disease, he was awarded exclusive rights to one of the two toilet seats assigned to the crew!

I recall a story Rudford told me about something he did in civilian life which resulted in his being encouraged to go into the military service. It seems he lived in the back woods of Kentucky and spent one afternoon in his late teens picking wild berries. He got so many that he stored them in his white T-shirt stretched out at his waist line. In his enthusiasm to show his mom his berries, he returned home–but suddenly got a weird inspiration as he approached the kitchen door. He crushed the berries against his stomach and let them drop to the porch floor. Then he knocked on the door, and when his mom appeared, he clutched his berry-soaked T-shirt and moaned, "Mom, I've been shot!" With that, his mother dropped to the floor in a dead faint. In moments his dad appeared and proceeded to beat the hell out of his son. And then sent him to the recruiting office to join the Navy.

After a few months on the *Allegheny*, I was transferred to a sister-tug, the *Penobscot*. Memorable was a voyage to Newfoundland in February. I was at the helm as we passed through the Cape Cod Canal. The captain of the tug was at my side, breathing heavily over the wheel–a nervous wreck. I couldn't believe that I, the underling, felt totally confident while my superior was going to pieces. Somehow we made it safely through. With no women in sight at Naval Station Argentia, the off-duty crew decided to dance–with each other. My partner was burly Bill Tilley from Georgia. It turned out he was great on the dance floor!

My last assignment was aboard a cable-layer after which my tour of duty ended. My parting memory of the Navy is a grim one. Ever since I have been wary of dentists. Before mustering out we had to have a complete physical. My only problem was one cavity. I stood in line for at least an hour (you get used to that in the service) awaiting my turn. Finally I was in the chair at about 4:30 p.m. It was well past the usual quitting time for the dentist and his unsmiling face showed it. His eyes were steel grey and his jaw was firmly set as I gazed up into his face. The drill was in his hand and soon I heard it burrowing its way into my jaw. I had never been so tense. And then the drill stuck a nerve, and I let go with a shriek which resounded into the hallways. The dentist's response? Through clenched teeth he shouted "SHUT UP!" Tears welled in my eyes as I winced in pain, but eventually it was all over. When I staggered out of the room, I noticed the frightened looks on those who were awaiting their turn.

Once out of the active service, there was the obligation of Naval Reserve duty which meant drill meetings periodically until my four years' obligation ended.

I wasn't the last Staats to enter military service. My son, Grant, is now a Captain in the Navy SEALS with some thirty years of service behind him. Grandson Zachary graduated from the Air Force Academy and is now studying for his Masters' Degree at Wright Patterson Air Base in Ohio. Grandson Evan is in the Navy learning how to diffuse bombs.

I have no regrets about service duty and heartily recommend it to any young person going through the decision making process in her/his formative years.

There were so many benefits. Getting to know people from all around the country and from all walks of life was the main benefit to me. You really get to know someone when you share close living quarters with then. It was also a great opportunity to experience some travel and to get away from the routine–but in a controlled environment. Learning discipline and a respect for order (I'm still sloppy at home, however) cannot be over emphasized. Patriotism and respect for the military were imbued in my allegiances. Then, too, I had the financial advantage of using the GI bill to complete both my Bachelors and Masters Degrees.

The Importance of Enduring Friendships

Being brought up and spending life in the same geographic area has its advantages. One is the possibility to make lifelong friends. It has been my good luck to keep close contact with at least a dozen people with whom I've been friends for approximately seventy years. A few are from my early childhood and several others I've known since elementary school. There were others gathered from Navy days and many with whom I became acquainted through friends and family as well as in my teaching career. The secret to these enduring relationships is to recognize that you can always find something in common (mutual interests, memories, etc.) even though your personal lives have drifted apart.

The main challenge is to make a concerted effort to keep in touch with those whose company you enjoy. Recently, in my 83rd year, I had lunch with a friend from elementary school days some 75 years ago. It just so happened his son-in-law worked at the college where I taught and that he wanted one of the books I had written. At our lunch conversation, he asked about my home town and asked if by any chance I knew his father-in-law. I sure did. We performed in high school operettas together. It had been 40 years since we had contact. When we got together I learned from lunch with my elderly former classmate that he'd become an attorney with an interest in protecting eminent domain rights. In spite of the huge gap in time since last seeing each other, we immediately poured through a list of teachers we remembered from our childhood. Since then, we maintain contact, mainly by E-Mail.

Traditional Party Get-togethers

Being part owner of our family homestead facilitated maintaining friendships. After high school, a favorite way for contact was through an annual Halloween party. A core of a dozen friends got together every late October. We would usually be joined by others for a fun evening. So many memories of unusual costumes! Of course, some of the games were repeated over the years: charades, pin the tail on the donkey, etc., but we often spliced in something as active as a scavenger hunt. We also explored the talents of various attendants.

One guy was so adept at *A Toast to Cardinal Puff* that his showmanship was demanded year after year. Another friend would illustrate how a colorful character had problems blowing out a candle.

The scavenger hunts were wild adventures. Days in advance, treasures were hidden at various locations in or near the homestead, with written clues as to their location. Teams worked against each other to see who could find the most hidden objects and also return with the loot. My most embarrassing recollection was the time the clue was flawed and some team members swam–in the dark frigid waters in late October–to a location (a lighthouse along the Hudson) which had been designated in error. I'd hidden the treasure at a lighthouse connected to the mainland by concrete dyke, but the clue gave a different lighthouse which was out in the river. When the team got back, some ugly words were spoken but all of us mellowed as we sipped beverages around the fireplace.

In another instance brother Larry and I plotted a surprise for the guests. We had found an old but sturdy wooden chair along the river bank some weeks earlier and set it near the fireplace as a prop. A guest, one of the wives at the Halloween party, chose the wooden chair for a seat. Well into the evening, as planned in advance, Larry declared when things were at a lull, "Bill, the fire is getting low. How about adding some wood?" Whereupon I asked the gullible guest to get up off the chair. Nearby I had hidden an axe, which I unveiled and proceeded to wield into a chopping spree that reduced the chair to splinters, which were casually tossed into the fire. Needless to say, a hush came over the room and awed silence prevailed until one long-time friend realized it was just another trick to liven up the evening.

In those days my friends and I were all young with budding families and not a hell of a lot of money, so it was the custom to charge a reasonable fee to attendants. The annual Halloween parties continued from 1952 through 1978. When one of the regular attendants passed away in his early 60s we ended the tradition in his memory. His specialty was donning a top hat and cane and belting out *Bill Bailey Won't You Please Come Home,* to the accompaniment of me on the piano.

Another long-lasting tradition which kept so many friends in touch was the annual Christmas party. It began in 1956 and has lasted through 2015 so far, a total of 59 years. The original attendance was only a dozen, but the crowd has swelled to well over 80 in recent years. For several decades it has been held at the homestead with the hosts providing punch and sandwiches and guests bringing along snacks and desserts and additional liquid refreshments. Among the many guests are children and grandchildren of the original attendants.

The program has stayed about the same: conversation spliced in between rounds of caroling and singing old favorites around the piano. Often a guest will offer extra entertainment by playing an instrument or joining in a combo. Along with the favored carols of *Silent Night, Adeste Fidelis, Little Town of Bethlehem* etc. are more modern holiday songs such as *Rudolph the Red-Nosed Reindeer, Frosty the Snowman,* and *Jingle Bells.* We often launch into old favorites like *Home on the Range, Red River Valley,* and *On Top of Old Smokey.* It's invariably a fun evening lasting over four hours, with some of the more spirited staying overnight. What a terrific way to catch up on developments and to talk over old times. We have competition with small groups singing verses of *The Twelve Days of Christmas,* and an old favorite is *Silver Bells* with the audience divided into two parts to voice the main verse and counterpart.

For some 30 years, we hosted summer theme parties on the lawns with a live band or DJ to provide entertainment and dance music. The parties took weeks to organize. Often a huge rented tent protected the attendants from glaringly hot sunlight or pattering rain. Flaming tiki torches added to the evening atmosphere. Portable toilets were rented. Sometimes a caterer was hired, but more often the main course was cooked over a charcoal fire. A few times, a pig roast provided the meat, and one time we roasted a side of beef. Fresh corn and salads were always a staple. It was part of the preparation to make a drive to New Hampshire where sales-tax-free booze could be bought cheaply. Kegs of beer were purchased locally.

At first the outdoor parties had a few dozen invitees. On one occasion, attendants were asked to attend in formal attire to sip champagne and sample appetizers before the main course and dancing. On another occasion hula dancing lessons were provided by a Hawaiian friend. At yet another party, line dancing and *The Macarena* were taught by experienced attendees.

As the summer parties grew in attendance, themes became very popular. Invitees were expected to wear theme costumes and activities were designed to embrace the theme. For instance, at the pirate theme party the scavenger hunt culminated in locating a hidden treasure chest. There was a Nautical theme party, a '50s party (think Elvis), and a Hawaiian party complete with stripped-to-the-waste fire spear throwers.

More than once the party featured a Viking funeral. In an ancient Scandinavian tradition, when a seafaring man passed away, he was placed in his fishing boat which was then set afire and cast out to sea For us this involved locating a sacrificial wooden boat which was never hard to find at the homestead. A straw dummy was laid in the boat. When darkness fell kerosene was sprinkled on *the deceased* and alighted. The boat was then pushed out into the river and set adrift. On one occasion, an attendant who was also ranked high among the New York State Troopers, excused himself and left the party when the flames lit up the river. He didn't want to be anywhere nearby if the police arrived in response to a phone call by a concerned neighbor from across the river. The last of the Viking funerals had to be cut short when, out of the night, a huge oil tanker plowed up the river as the burning boat drifted toward the channel. That required an energetic swimming and dousing spree.

The festive summer parties grew and grew in attendance until the point where the crowd seemed unmanageable in spite of gate security, efforts to police behavior, etc. The final party was a beauty featuring one popular local band, *The Refrigerators* who had become personal friends of Uncle Barry. The ambience was great, the music and dancing were phenomenal, but there were just too many attendants to keep track of, and a dangerous situation could have developed. After that scare it was decided to end the big summer bashes and continue on only with smaller group celebrations.

BACHELOR PARTIES

In the '50s and '60s many of our family and friends were in their 20s. Predictably, weddings abounded. What better place to have a bachelor part than at the homestead. Over the years there must have been dozens of them. Most often they were beer parties with plenty of sports activities including softball, billiards, croquet and swimming.

Traditionally, one or two full kegs of beer were on tap with a variety of snacks paid for by attendants sharing equally (with the exception of the groom).

The festivities would often start at noon with the group assembled on the softball field for a vigorous game and with a pickup truck loaded with beer and ice nearby. Many parties were evening affairs with the billiard table as the main focus. Sometimes, croquet matches were so engrossing that outdoor electric lights had to be used when darkness closed in.

Sometimes things got a little out of hand. The village of Castleton three miles south of the homestead had five bar rooms, and occasionally the bachelor party would find its boundaries extended beyond the homestead. One time It so happened that the deputy sheriff in charge of the town had quit his job just prior to one of the parties. It also just so happened that one of the party invitees was the type who became belligerent after a few beers. Bad combination! The party had adjourned to a Castleton bar after the softball game ended.

All was going along normally on that warm summer evening when a uniformed Marine Corps enlistee entered the pub. For some reason our belligerent friend, an ex-Navy man, resented this Marine who was a total stranger to him. The next thing we all knew, a brawl complete with fisticuffs erupted between the Marine and our ex-Navy pal. The bartender ushered us out onto the street, whereupon brother Barry, in John Wayne-like fashion, stepped into the circle surrounding the fighting twosome. With authority he shouted, "Stand back all of you," and with that the crowd disbursed and the fighting subsided. As we departed the scene in our respective vehicles, the future bridegroom, a normally placid sort, wanted me to stop at a nearby brickyard, load my car trunk with bricks, drive back past the bar and pitch bricks though the window! Now, wouldn't that have been a memorable experience.

Only on one occasion was a woman involved, and that was totally harmless in terms of moral behavior. It was a night time party and a dozen or so guys arrived, expecting the usual entertainment of beer drinking, darts, and billiards. Not this time! Unknown to any of the rest of us, one of the party planners hired a stripper. I recall that brother Barry was nursing an aching shoulder that evening, but was hanging in there just to be sociable.

The girl arrived unobtrusively dressed in casual attire and she joined in the fun of playing billiards and darts. We all thought her presence was odd but assumed she was a girlfriend of one of the guests and that she was just joining us for an hour or so of fun. Then she disappeared from the scene and a few minutes later we were all encouraged to take a seat in the living room around the fire. Next came some fanfare musical recording and the door to another section of the house opened. Our mystery guest burst in among us, almost naked–hips, and boobs swinging. Wow, was she attractive–and boy could she dance!

When she passed close enough by, it was expected that the guests would crush a folded dollar bill into the elastic of her panties. The entertainment was very much appreciated. Brother Barry, whom I thought was suffering from the pain in his shoulder, got down on his hands and knees and asked the young lady to play *horsey* by riding on his back. So much for the wounded shoulder!

After about a half hour of the strip act, the young lady was escorted away from the party by whoever had the bright idea to invite her in the first place. In hindsight, the evening was a fun change of pace.

Brother Larry held off marriage until age 54. He was engineer in the merchant marine, signing up for a ship when he got the urge to earn some money. The ship found itself anchored near Alesund, Norway, for several months with the Arab oil crisis of the '70s idled just about all of our fuel-carrying fleet. There he met a Norwegian shipping clerk and eventually asked her to marry him. His wedding was in Norway, but the bachelor party took place at the homestead. Several guys sipped vodka shots from noon until dawn. In the warm summer evening, people just dropped onto the lawn when they tired. The next morning the hillside resembled the battlefield at Antietam with the bodies scattered about in disarray.

WEDDINGS, ANNIVERSARIES, ETC.

In the 50s, most of the wedding receptions took place at banquet halls in the Albany area. They were delightful occasions with lots of great food and fine dancing. At brother Bleeck's wedding, the music traditionally followed the banquet. Toward the end of the evening, the attendees gathered on the dance floor in a huge circle surrounding the newlyweds and sang *Let Me Call You Sweetheart* as they danced together. Since the bride and groom had no car and were heading to Jersey City for the honeymoon, we drove them to the railroad station in Albany. We waved them off as they boarded the train while continuing singing the *Sweetheart* refrain.

At a subsequent wedding reception in the same facility, a different type of memorable occasion took place. I had been seeing a lovely girl for some time, and we were both invited to the wedding. Before the banquet, a group of us were having drinks and finger foods and I gallantly offered to go to the bar and get a drink for my date. When I got to the bar, the 60+ mother of a good friend was seated on a stool enjoying a whiskey sour.

"What are you doing?" she inquired of me.

"Ordering my girl a drink," I responded.

"Ordering your girl a drink," she sneered at me and then continued by saying, "And what are you, an errand boy—a Mr. Milquetoast?"

Then she said, "Don't be in such a hurry. Sit down here with me and we'll enjoy a drink together." She proceeded to order two whiskey sours. And following that, two more. About an hour later, I staggered back to my table and faced more than the music from the dance band.

I recall one of my daughter's wedding reception at the homestead following the wedding ceremony at the church. It was a beautiful summer day and we had hired a caterer who provided the tent, tables and chairs, food—the works. Even fancy linen tablecloths.

With so many young attendants, things were bound to get exciting as the liquid refreshments were consumed. My son, Grant's, best friend had borrowed his brother's suit for the occasion, and he said repeatedly how important it was to return the suit in good condition. As the evening became a blur, I recall someone heaving a piece of wedding cake at the suited guest who, enraged, proceeded to chase the culprit across clean linen table tops and through wet grass—snorting in anger as he closed in on the prey. *The prey* was desperate to remain alive and managed to escape his thundering hate-filled former friend. Needless to say, the suit was a mess. And the outcome with the linen tablecloths? The caterer refused to take them back and charged extra for the damage.

The occasion was also noteworthy for the swimming prowess of several in the wedding party, clad in evening dresses and tuxes.

At another wedding celebration a conga line was formed to the tune of *I Heard It Through the Grape Vine*. The line snaked across the riverfront dance floor and into the Hudson, clothes and all. Fortunately these were rented gowns. I can still see my daughter, disappearing under the surface wearing her tiara!

Yet another wedding ceremony took place on the riverside diving platform, a sturdy structure some ten feet above the water level complete with a 30-foot access ramp and diving board. Spectators stood on the dance deck at the river's edge and also on the grassy lawn. No one planned it, of course, but during the ceremony a tour boat cruised by, loaded with gawking passengers who could see the ceremony in progress. That's when the cat calls resounded from the boat, among them: "Don't do it, you fool", "Jump!" and "You'll be sorry." Interestingly enough, that omen portended a marriage that lasted only a few years.

Another ill-fated marriage occurred on a scorching July day in the middle of drought which turned the lawns brown. During the outdoor ceremony, a dog followed the bride up the aisle and proceeded to empty its bowels mid-vows. Another omen of a failed marriage.

Son Grant's summer wedding was romantically inspirational as he met his beautiful bride in white while dressed in his immaculately clean Naval Officers uniform.

My niece, Monica's wedding was wonderful. The grass was green, the sun shone and the temperatures were moderately warm on a beautiful July day. Weeks of work had gone into preparation. Lawns were trimmed, festive lights were installed, and a large tent was erected along with smaller ones.

The wedding itself had only a few dozen attendees and consisted of an intimate morning ceremony performed on the dancing deck at river's edge. In mid-afternoon, some 120 casually dressed guests of all ages arrived, bringing snacks, salads and desserts to supplement the corn and chicken and beer provided by the bride and groom. Family members manned the grills and self-service food was provided.

Following the banquet, a 15-piece ensemble of only drums provided uniquely enjoyable rhythm for an hour or so. Spectators joined in the fun by dancing wildly, and some even took up hand clackers to supplement the drums

As darkness closed in, an amazing fireworks display took place. Following that, a huge bonfire was started in the outdoor fireplace. With no wind to blow sparks, all was under control. A DJ had been hired to provide for dancing on the riverside deck, with the floor packed to capacity by dozens of lively participants. The DJ played past midnight, with one of the closing selections, *Take It to the Limit* by the Eagles giving several a burst of energy to sing along with an old favorite from the '80s.

Dozens of attendants had set up tents rather than taking a chance on driving home under the influence of alcohol. Several of them, in spite of a foggy reaction from the wedding festivities, pitched in to help clean up the debris the following morning.

BIRTHDAY BASHES

Some birthday celebrations are especially memorable. When brother Larry reached 75, it was decided to give him a surprise party. Some 80 guests attended, including many of his old friends who had moved to distant locations. The party was truly a surprise. I was sure he would soon realize this wasn't just another festive occasion once a few old friends showed up. He remained oblivious until his wife said, "Larry, don't you have any idea what this party is all about?" He didn't but it became very obvious once the program started and tributes were made.

When brother Barry's 80th came up, it was time for yet another festive celebration. The surprise element on this occasion was to have one of our attractive young lady friends burst out of a huge birthday cake. It took weeks of effort and considerable ingenuity to prepare the huge cardboard cake large enough to hide an adult inside. Not only that–the cake had to be hidden out of sight until well into the party when the guests were at their merriest. Daughter Giss came up with the idea of building a platform on the back of a lawn mower cart which could be driven to the unveiling sight. Planks were put in place and the cardboard cake, constructed, painted and decorated, was set on top of the platform.

An hour before the surprise unveiling, there was a glitch. The young lady who agreed to bounce out of the cake got cold feet and refused to take part. She would be just too embarrassed. What to do? With a few gin and tonics under my belt, I got up the courage to volunteer my services instead. It would be ugly but it sure would be a surprise. Somewhere in a closet I found a tattered bright red evening dress. With heavy makeup and earrings and a wig, the outfit was complete.

At about midnight, Giss drove the lawnmower near the heart of the party where cheers and applause greeted the arriving cake. Barry was handed a knife and was about to cut the cake when the top burst open and out I sprang–smothering my brother with lipstick-smeared kisses. He had no idea that it was me! He kept wondering for hours who the hag was. That party will linger on in memories for decades.

OTHER SOCIAL OCCASIONS

Spliced among all of the special, more formalized get-togethers with friends and family over the years have been innumerable social occasions, not specifically designed to reinforce friendships, but surely that has been a side effect. After high school graduation and military service, there could have been little to bind family and friends together, but efforts to keep in touch have done just that.

Young families evolved. During those years most of our social occasions involved parties at various homes. Sometimes it was in the form of an outdoor picnic with children. Often we played cards: pinochle gatherings and also occasional poker sessions for the guys.

In later years, when the children grew old enough to be left alone, we adults took advantage of our freedom and ventured forth on travel vacations together. It was fun to rent a moped for an autumn day at Martha's Vineyard and find a secluded beach where we could enjoy wine and cheese. We repeated the process at Nantucket and on Block Island. And, too, there was that unique vacation where we rented a Cape Cod cottage which had beautiful white swans swimming on a nearby pond. After a dinner at home, six of us gathered on the porch to watch the setting sun and sip wine. Someone forgot to close an outside door, and when a visit was made to go inside the house, two swans were found to be wandering around in the living room! To add to the memory of it all, a faucet broke and water just about flooded us out until the turn-off valve was discovered.

I hate shopping–absolutely abhor it. So what do the majority of my fellow travelers choose to do on a sunny seaside day? Shop–and at the damned Christmas Tree Shop to boot. There are four of them at various locations on the Cape, every damned one of them carrying the same line of merchandise. Nevertheless, we had to visit each one. The worst was when we stopped to shop at the grand prize: the biggest Christmas Tree Shop of them all at Hyannis. I seethed, but I complied, just to keep peace.

For a change of pace, we did group visits to Connecticut's Foxwood Casino. One time there were six of us in the van, and for some reason we got hopelessly lost. Fred Hutchinson, the driver, made a unique suggestion: "I'm going to follow the car ahead of us," he said. "It is full of Asians, and we all know that Asians like to gamble, so they must be headed for the casino." Follow them we did–right into their driveway as they maneuvered their car into their garage!

Odd things seemed to happen to this long-standing group of friends. When the son of one of the group decided to marry, I volunteered to book a motel in upstate New Jersey for several of us. Since it was summer, I specifically asked if they had a swimming pool, and they replied in the affirmative. When we got there we saw the pool. It was empty! I angrily approached the motel receptionist. "You told me on the phone that you had a pool, and the one here is dry as a bone." Her response: "When you asked for a pool, you didn't ask if there was water in it."

We booked elsewhere.

Once in a while in those years, the guys would meet at a local bar for a few beers. Remember that in those days, DWI's were not yet in force. Yes, we drove impaired, but with good fortune there were never any serious accidents.

It was often such a treat just to change the pace, and there have been so many treasured memories of the fun. For instance, there was the night of bar hopping in Rensselaer with three or four long-term friends. We wound up at the Fort Crailo Inn sometime around 2 a.m. The bartender handed me a beer and in my hazy condition, I let the glass slip through my fingers and smash on the floor. For some reason, the bartender blamed himself and apologized, saying, "I'm sorry. That was careless of me. Here, let me pour you another," whereupon he turned on the tap and poured me another beer. I reached out in his direction, attempted to grasp the glass, and once again failed to maintain my grip. The glass followed its predecessor, falling to the floor and crashing.

"That's it! You're out of here," the bartender bellowed, pointing to the door. That was the end of that party.

Then there was the occasion where I nearly wound up in jail. Albany used to be a tough town in the 1950s. Now and then I would join brother Larry and a few friends for a night out. One time we slugged down several beers at a dive called the *Times Square* on Hudson Avenue in downtown Albany. Let me tell you, that was one rough crowd. A muscular tattooed woman churned her hips to the *Dirty Boogie* as we looked on with amazement.

Off to the side, I noticed a guy becoming loudly obnoxious. The tough looking Italian lady who tended bar repeatedly warned the guy to tone it down. He persisted. It wasn't long before the barroom door burst open and two police officers strode in. They made their way directly to the culprit, and proceeded to belt him unconscious with a black jack. I'd never seen one of those before! Then they dragged the guy to the waiting police car and that was the end of him for the night. Foggy minded and in deep admiration for the tough bartender's show of authority, I blurted out in a loud voice: "Rosa!"–this in reference to a radio show at the time, *Life with Luigi* where one of the characters had that name.

She abruptly turned to me and responded, "You're next!" Whereupon my brother and I sipped the rest of our beer dry and then made it for the door.

Life Long Friends

In the past 83 years there have been so many close relationships that it's impossible to rank them as to who would be the closest. The fact is that all of them have (or in some cases, had) remained close associates for several decades. With me, once a friendship became close, it morphed into a lifelong commitment. To cite several that lasted more than forty years:

BOB CURRIER

I met Bob Currier the day I walked into my high school home room in September of 1946. Our school system was set up so that those of us who lived at the lower end of the city attended the first eight grades at an elementary school in the neighborhood. There were two other elementary school in the city. We would then all be sent to the high school for grades nine through twelve. I would say that, at that point, my social life began.

It's a wonder we became friends. Bob was athletic--good at basketball, baseball, softball and just about any other sport he attempted.

In sports, I was hopeless. I believe in my entire high school career, I sunk only one basketball into the hoop to earn two points—and that was at the mercy of the gym coach. That landmark achievement came after the whistle for ending the scrimmage came and the coach said, "Staats, after seeing you struggle for four years at intermural basketball, I want you to have those two points because I've been watching your hopeless efforts and I think you deserve the break!"

Bob's love life was enviable. Being an attractive curly haired blonde athlete, the girls swarmed around him. Not me; every date was only after agonizing over whether or not to ask for one. I was so damned afraid to be rejected.

His family background was not all that enviable. His biological father and his mom divorced when Bob was very young, and his Mom had remarried poorly, tying up with a guy who drank too much and ran a tavern. His mother was stalwart, however. She became his sole provider when he was a teenager. What a strong lady! Before she retired she worked at a loom in a local woolen mill which was a physically demanding job and boring as hell. She was sharp-witted and inclined to let you know exactly how she felt about issues and people—and she had very strong opinions. I suspect she dropped out of school, but that didn't diminish her wisdom. I loved her. The bill of fare at dinnertime was usually potato chips and baloney sandwiches. We became good friends for years and I'm sure that had to do with her spunk.

On the personality side, Bob was somewhat conceited and would appear to have a barrier around him. I think it was because of his family situation. Deep inside he was a genuinely good guy, enjoying fun and very mindful of his friendship commitments.

Bob was one of a number of my high school colleagues and we grew closer as the years went by. Our first project together was to tarpaper the leaking roof of a shed his mom had in the back yard. It took only an afternoon and were admiring our handiwork when the job was completed. At that point, his mother appeared.

"Great job, boys, I really appreciate it!" his mother remarked and then made a startling observation. "Do you notice that you put the tarpaper upside down and that the seams overlap in the wrong direction? When it rains, it will still leak." The proper alignment of the seams never occurred to us. Nevertheless, we left the job as it was, but we joked about it ever so frequently.

We spent a lot of our teen years together, often just idling, listening to hit tunes on the radio or enjoying casual nights in front of the fire at the homestead with other buddies.

One time I asked him to join my mother and I and brother Larry on a trip to Buffalo in the summertime, riding in the Model A Ford. I asked him the day before we were headed west. "I'd really like to join you but I don't have any money," he said. I didn't have much, either.

Then he had a thought: "Maybe I can get into a card game this afternoon. If I win I'll phone you. It'll be fun." Sure as hell, he won and we were off. The ride wasn't all that great. It rained and we had two flat tires. Not only that, Bob and I were relegated to riding in the rumble seat which was open to the weather and we had to protect ourselves under a soggy blanket. The trip took 11 hours and we were glad to arrive at my sister's home in Buffalo.

Once in Buffalo, my brother-in-law, Hans, gave us an insight into the adult life ahead of us, including cocktails, burlesque show—and also a trip to see Niagara Falls

When I joined the Navy, we went our separate ways but kept in touch when we had occasional leaves at the same time. I was an attendant in his wedding in 1954 and extremely pleased that he had met a terrific girl while attending the business college. The prenuptial activities were most memorable. Ronnie's dad owned a guide boat moored at Hague in upper Lake George. After hours at the local pub, several of us took a hair-raising midnight ride on the lake. Needless to say, most of us were subdued the next day for the wedding ceremony.

It wasn't long after Bob's wedding that I met my future bride. By this time most of my buddies had married and at age 25, I was the last of the group to make the wedding vows. A year later, our children began appearing and that process went on for a dozen years or so. In the meantime, Bob and Ronnie and Sandy and I and a few other couples were in continuous touch through card games, picnics, evenings out, etc. There were children to be cared for but that became a part of the routine. Then in later years, our children found marriage partners and we maturing parents joined in on the wedding celebrations. After that came grandchildren. Ours was an idyllic relationship for decades.

When Bob was only 54, he was in a minor automobile accident and I believe he fell out of the driver's seat of his car and suffered a head injury. That may not have been the cause of his declining health thereafter but it certainly is plausible. At any rate, Bob's memory began to fail and within a few months, despite a number of experimental treatments, Alzheimer's took over his life.

As the years passed, Ronnie stood by him, giving constant care. They moved to Florida so that Bob could get out for walks in the winter. Twelve years of grueling decline ensued. Eventually, Ronnie could no longer manage the care and Bob was placed in a senior facility.

The sad part is that Bob knew he had Alzheimer's and what the future held. I recall a conversation we had when he was in the early stages. "I feel useless–I'm like a store mannequin." It was heartbreaking to visit him. In his mid-sixties, my buddy passed away. Once again I am blessed with fond memories of a good friend and have maintained a close relationship with Ronnie all through the years since Bob's passing. I try to spend a few days with her in Florida each winter and she reciprocates by staying with me for a while in the summer while renewing her other friendships up north.

BILL (BEAKY) GRAHAM

Another terrific buddy of mine, Bill Graham, preferred to be called *Beaky* with reference to his prominent nose in which he took great pride. We met in the fourth grade but didn't become buddies until high school. He had a great sense of humor. In his teen years he became quite an outdoorsman, interested mainly in hunting and fishing. His grandfather kept bees and Beak helped out. It was Beak who had the clubhouse in his back yard where several high school colleagues would gather in the colder months to listen to the *Billboard* magazine top ten songs every Saturday morning.

In our senior year in high school, we drove the Model A Ford roadster to Cape Cod– in March. Beak had met a girl there the previous summer and was sure her folks would be delighted to see us. The drive took forever because there was no interstate highways at the time. In addition, the Model A cruised at a whopping 37 miles an hour. When we got to the Cape, neither the girl nor her folks were at home and so we sought out other accommodation in which to spend the night. A motel was out of the question because we barely had money for gas.

We located an unoccupied tourist cabin on the beach and were able to access it through an unlocked window. The electricity was turned off and by that time it was getting dark, so we were forced to go to bed at eventide. It was so damned cold that we slept between two mattresses with our overcoats on.

We were awakened early the next morning by a loud knocking on the door. It was the police.

"We received a phone call stating that there were two suspicious characters in a beat up car at this cottage. We could haul you guys off to jail, but instead will let you go if you promise to be off the Cape by noon. That was the end of our Cape Cod adventure.

Beak and I joined the Navy reserve at the time of the Korean War and we did our summer training at a camp in Maryland. Our Navy orders didn't indicate whether to wear the heavy woolen blue uniform or the whites. We did not consider the hot and humid temperatures in Maryland in summer and chose to wear the wool fabric blues.

Not only did we have to put up with the heat, but we had to do physical exercises all day long.

After high school, we each did the obligatory full time Navy service for two years. Beak served on the aircraft carrier, *Antietam*. When our service was over we resumed hanging out together, I introduced him to our next door homestead neighbor, Mary Podoba, and they struck up a close relationship calling each other *Jake* all through the years. Two years later they married. In the meantime Mary introduced me to her close friend, Evie Ray, and we hit it off and frequently double dated with Beak and Mary.

Beak and Mary had two sons. He worked as a lineman for the phone company and Mary worked in a research lab. They lived in a trailer adjacent to Mary's parents' home. In later years, they bought a vacation home at Cape Hatteras. This gave Beak a chance to surf fish or fish from his boat to his heart's content. The Outer Banks are precarious during hurricane season, but their home has remained unscathed for several decades.

He also became partner in the ownership of a hunting lodge deep in the Adirondacks. After retirement Beak and Mary moved to the Winston-Salem area in North Carolina nearby their son, Gary, an anesthetist. I have enjoyed visiting them over the past several years. Mary and I have been friends for more than 70 years!

Fred Hutchinson

Another fun associate for more than sixty years has been Fred Hutchinson. I met him through Bob Currier. We didn't attend school together because he was sent to a military school, CBA probably because his folks thought he needed the discipline.

It's Fred's self-deprecating sense of humor that has played a major role in our relationship. His dad ran a tavern in upper Rensselaer–an oasis for us young singles who loved to drink beer and shoot darts. In 1955 Fred married Peg Hall from Hudson, NY, and it was at about that time when, as young married couples, Fred, Bob Currier and Bill Reimann, together with a few others, developed a continuous relationship.

Fred had three sisters and he was the only boy, so while growing up he was treated like a king by his folks–and it spilled over into his married life when Peg became the patient partner.

There have been so many incidents when Fred has provided our group with laughs. There was that vacation when three couples went to Cape Cod. After we were seated in one restaurant, Fred excused himself to go to the men's room. In his absence we ordered breakfast. When Fred returned to the table he asked, "did anyone remember to order my juice?" For those of us used to his being pampered, this was really funny and we derided him for it unmercifully.

When we finally reached home, Fred had a parting message for me. "Please don't plan on stopping in for a while, because there's a football game on TV that I'd rather watch than talk to you." Since I think watching football is a most boring pastime I shot back, "Fred,

I'm out of here like a bullet. I wouldn't be caught dead spending even a few more dull minutes with you."

Over the years, Fred and I have shared scores of social occasions. There was brother Larry's bachelor party at the homestead when we all did vodka shots until dawn while standing on the lawn overlooking the river. "I guess I don't ever remember watching the sun come up when I was having a hangover," Fred commented.

Fred was there when we had yet another beer party at the homestead. I had invited a few teaching colleagues from Hudson High. One of the attendants considered himself to be an excellent golfer and demonstrated it in the most bizarre fashion. He had his close friend, who was drunk, lay on the lawn, a golf tee in his teeth with a golf ball balanced on it. The *expert* daringly swung his club. He so easily could have missed but instead connected perfectly sending the ball half way across the river. We were all astounded by the fete and relieved, too, that the guest was still alive!

Ours has been an enjoyable friendship what with continuous ribbing on both sides. There was that time Fred was having a new home built in Schodack. Typically, Fred had a tendency to run out of patience--this time around with the building contractor whom he fired. Then he became distressed because autumn was coming and the house had to be finished. Fred phoned several friends to come out and help him shingle the roof. I was one of those he called. When I arrived at his place, he said, "I never in my life thought that I would be so desperate as to call on you for help." He was good at back-handed compliments.

It was Fred who persuaded a group of us while on a Montreal weekend, to visit a dive called, *La Sex Machine*. The place turned out to be Sodom and Gomorrah-like with bosom-shaped upholstery, phallic posts, glass tables held up by spread legs, lewd ceiling art, and the bartender and waitresses scantily clad. The women in our group were not at all happy and insisted upon leaving. Fred got the brunt of the flack which he so richly deserved.

Some years ago, Fred and Peg sold their home and moved to Florida. As a golf nut, it was inevitable that he would reside abutting a golf course. In the summer, they lived in a trailer park not far from the Saratoga race track where he and Peg had part time jobs. He kept the computers in shape and Peg worked as a ticket salesperson.

Fred is no dummy. He completed college part time while working as a pay phone toll collector. He went on to sell computer software for NEC and was a representative in Japan. He also did some part time teaching.

Fred and Peg had two girls and a boy who all turned out to be fine adults with great senses of humor. Each of them found terrific partners. They have been very good to their folks. In his later years, when he needed kidney dialysis, his daughter and husband opened their home to he and Peg for several months. We still talk on the phone but visiting has become more difficult.

BILL REIMANN

Bill Reimann was my brother-in-law. He became a close friend through frequent family contacts. I first knew Bill because his wife-to-be, Marcia, was the friend of a friend from high school. When he and Marcia married, they asked his sister, Sandy, and I, to be attendants. Bill and Marcia became companions through family events. He and I liked to compete at croquet and also at the billiard table. Also, we both enjoyed playing poker.

Sandy and I and Bill and Marcia usually spent a few days together at Upper Saranac Lake, where Sandy's and Bill's sister Jean and her husband had built a summer camp. Those fun years lasted more than two decades. Jean's camp was huge, with five bedroom and wide screened-in porch overlooking the lake. Summer fun included boating, swimming, water skiing and gathering around the outdoor fireplace in the evening. We built solid friendships with the entire Thompson family–Jean and Stan and their daughter and four sons.

In his late sixties, Bill developed melanoma which went undetected and was not treated properly. He had some chemotherapy, but died in the spring unexpectedly.

RAY DODSON

I met Ray Dodson while in the Navy on my first assignment aboard the sea-going tug, *Allegheny*. He'd previously been in the Navy and had been discharged and put on reserve duty status. When the Korean War broke out he was recalled to active service.

Ray was a fun drinking companion and we enjoyed each other's company so much that I asked him to come home with me on those weekends we were stationed at the Brooklyn Navy yard. He loved upstate New York and fell for a gal in my Rensselaer neighborhood.

Before being recalled into the service, Ray had been a coal miner from near Johnstown, PA. For years he had labored underground with a pick and shovel. His dad died from black lung disease and Ray grew up in very Spartan circumstances with his mom and younger sister.

On my first visit to his home, I was arrested! In my snappy 1941 Ford convertible, I didn't notice the speed trap near Crescent. The policeman asked for a $5 fine and I lied and told him I was broke.

"In that case, I'll take you to Ebensburg jail where you will be hoeing potatoes for the rest of the summer" he assured me. I phoned Ray and he came and rescued me by paying the fine. The arrest became a standing joke for years.

Ray and I and some other crew members had a great time drinking in San Juan, Puerto Rico. In hindsight I think I might better have spent my time sightseeing, but those social outings enabled me to make more friends.

After active duty in the navy, Ray and I kept in touch. He went to the University of Pittsburgh to become a mining engineer and I went back to Albany State College for Teachers. Eventually Ray worked his way up to become an executive with Bethlehem Steel. He was an excellent administrator because he knew the business by starting at the bottom working shoulder to shoulder with the miners.

Ray married Sophie, a local girl who taught in an elementary school. They had six children. Sandy and I had seven. One summer we took the whole brood on vacation to Hammonasset beach in Connecticut. Sophie loved to cook and was looking forward to making feasts for all of us. Unfortunately, I had rented cheap cabins which had only a countertop electric burner for cooking. We made the best of it. We spent the daytime at the beach and in the evening we would stuff all thirteen of the children into one cabin where they played games. In the other cabin next to where the children stayed, Ray and Sophie and Sandy and I played pinochle and enjoyed drinks.

One day, Ray and I gave the ladies a break by piling all of the kids into my station wagon and driving off to the trolley museum. At the museum they charged by the carload and the attendant was aghast when we showed up.

"You guys sure know how to get your money's worth," he commented.

Another time, we cleaned up the children and took them to a family restaurant. The rest of the time we lived on home-made meals and sandwiches. Our off-spring have since grown up to have families of their own. Ray retired after his brood graduated from college and not long after that Bethlehem Steel went into bankruptcy. Ray lost much of his pension and hospital benefits. Fortunately, Sophie's teaching pension and health insurance carried them through.

I still occasionally drive to western Pennsylvania to visit the Dodsons. Ray and I manage to communicate in spite of mutual hearing problems. A few years ago Ray and I drove to Newtown Bridge in West Virginia to see the bungie jumping and parachuting exhibitions. It's been more than sixty years since Ray and I met and I deeply appreciate his friendship.

RAY CALL

Yet another enduring relationship began when I met Ray Call at the Teachers' College. He was from down-state Rockland County and while in Albany he lived in a dorm, earning part of his sustenance by washing dishes. I commuted daily to the college from home.

We got to know each other when we pledged at the same fraternity. Once again, humor was the mutual attraction.

Pledging the fraternity involved hazing and I vividly remember being required to swallow some pills which turned my pee blue for several days.

One of the bullies hazing us was very proud to be from Orange County and called himself an OCB (Orange County Boy). "What is an OCB?" the bully shouted at a blindfolded me during the hazing. I had no idea how to respond but blurted out, "OutCast Bastard." Laughter rang out from all sides. Acceptance was assured.

Ray's folks were excellent hosts and I made it a point to visit them—even after Ray and I graduated. His dad had a wry sense of humor, and his mother was very friendly. She was active in local Republican politics. As *angels* they also invested in some successful Broadway theater productions.

One time I showed up at their home at 2 a.m. and, since the doors were locked, I sneaked through an un-locked basement window. In the dark I found my way to Ray's bedroom. The next morning they were really surprised to see me. "I wish I'd thought to bring the shotgun to bed with me," his dad commented.

His mother prided herself in her culinary skills. For a gag I once brought along a spoon with a fake fly glued to it. At breakfast, I stealthily slipped the *trick* spoon into Ray's cereal. When he saw the fly, he exclaimed, "Holy cow, there's a fly on my spoon." His mother was shocked beyond my expectations and chastened me for my surprise. Our relationship remained cordial, but when I left the Call homestead, his mother said, "We'd love to have you come back again put please, no spoons with flies."

Ray and I had an interesting experience at a drive-in theater in Rensselaer. The movie was great—but we were stopped by the police while exiting the theater.

"You are under arrest," he announced. "You backed your car into another customer's car. We know you did it because your Model A Ford is one of a kind. You are to report to the police station at 8 a.m. tomorrow."

"But I didn't do it," I reasoned.

Ray and I had been planning to spend the weekend with his folks and I didn't want to miss the opportunity.

"How can I get out of this? I didn't back into anyone's car and I can't see why I have to stick around to deny a false accusation."

The officer thought for a while and then said, "If you can persuade the accuser to phone the police station and withdraw the complaint against you, you can go on your way." By this time it was midnight.

I phoned the accuser's number given to me by the police. The phone must have rung at least a dozen times before he groggily picked it up.

"I'm the guy you are accusing of backing into your car at the drive in. I didn't do it. What color was the car that backed into yours?" "Black," he answered.

"My car is blue. Please phone the East Greenbush police station right now so that I can get on my way."

He did so, and Ray will never let me forget our near-jail experience.

One time we decided to go to his place on a cold winter Friday night. There was no interstate in those days so we drove Route 9W, a narrow, two-lane road. Then the snow started. It snowed and snowed and snowed–so much so that the windshield wipers in the Model A couldn't keep up. There were no side curtains on the car so the snow piled up on our laps. At our age it was challenging and fun and we'll never forgot leaning out the window and scraping snow off the windshield by hand.

I left the teachers' college after the first two years to join the Navy. Ray went into the Army and served as a security officer in Germany. Both of us returned to the college after our military careers. We resumed the friendship. Ray married a fellow classmate and they taught at a downstate high school. I married Sandy and taught in the Albany area.

Ray and I continued our relationship, usually with our wives along to enjoy the fun. He and his wife bought a mobile home in Florida after retirement, but shortly thereafter his wife Joyce contracted Parkinson's.

Fortunately, by this time their three children were fully grown and engaged in jobs. It was sad to see Joyce's health decline. She remained alert and sharp for many years, enjoying sports on TV. Joyce passed away recently, but Ray and I have kept in touch–nurturing a friendship now nearing its seventieth year

In my recent contact with Ray, he had not lost his sense of humor. He now lives in an assisted living facility north of Glens Falls. It seems the management got the idea to install a swimming pool, hoping it might attract a younger group of residents. A meeting was called of the residents in order to gather feedback on the new idea. There was considerable discussion and then Ray joined in with his viewpoint: "Most of the residents who will enjoy the pool are wearing depends— surely they won't get out of the pool when they have to relieve themselves." He was backed up by a fellow resident who ventured, "I suppose we could refer to the pool as *On Golden Pond*. That brand of humor really appeals to me.

Allen Hulls

In the winter of 1965 I decided to try for a teaching job in Australia. It was time to break away from the usual routine and I felt stuck in a rut. Amazingly, Sandy went along with the idea, in spite of having four young offspring. I made a contact with an Australian educator visiting Albany and he gave me the address of the

Royal Melbourne Institute of Technology (RMIT), a downtown comprehensive technical college with an enrollment of about 25,000. I wrote to the head of the school of business.

I couldn't believe that I would receive an offer but a confirming letter arrived, signed by Allen Hulls, Department Head, School of Accountancy. My family were on our way toward a one-year teaching gig in Melbourne, Australia's second largest city, which had a population at the time of more than two million.

Breaking into the Australian lifestyle wasn't easy. We knew no one. After two months, relationships with teaching colleagues developed–helped along by late Friday afternoon beer guzzling sessions. On Fridays, I usually took my car so that I could visit the Victoria Market downtown.

With the car, I felt free to drive my friends to my place so that they could meet Sandy. She was delighted to have the contact, even though we were slightly inebriated. I often had colleagues and their wives in for an evening of snacks, conversation, and some slides of the snow in upstate New York

I came to respect the department head, Allen Hulls. He was an excellent administrator. He grew up on a farm in Leongatha, some 50 miles east of Melbourne. He was an airman for Britain's RAF in WW11 piloting a Spitfire. He saw plenty of action and was even shot down over Germany and rescued by a resistance supporter. That was while he was in his late teens. After the war he graduated from the University of Melbourne and taught in high school for a few years. He took the job as department head in RMIT and the program grew rapidly.

I recall when our senses of humor first kicked in. I'd gone to his office and in the course of our conversation, I mentioned that my office was chilly in this damp and dreary Melbourne winter. His response, "You'll get used to it–you Yanks are soft."

"I wouldn't be soft if I had a nice toasty electric heater under my desk like I see under yours."

The friendship progressed. Sandy and I invited Allen and his wife, Elizabeth, to our home for dinner. I found the ingredients for blueberry pie, something Allen came to love when he was training to be a pilot in Montreal. For liquid refreshment Allen, as all Aussie guys, liked beer while Liz preferred brandy mixed with vermouth.

That was a night to remember what with some terrific conversation, laughter, and even dancing exhibitions.

Within a week, Elizabeth phoned to ask us to join them at a dinner-dance at the Club Alexander in downtown Melbourne. That was another memorable evening, complete with a nine-course dinner with dancing intervals. We had a joke telling fest and, unbelievably, the guys engaged in a pissing contest outside of the home of Allen's friend targeting a soon-to-wilt peach tree.

When summer came, Allen asked my whole family to spend the day at their vacation home on the beach of the Mornington Peninsula. Following a great day, the Hulls extended the invitations several more times.

When Sandy delivered daughter Heather in March of 1966, the Hulls gave us diaper (nappy) service for two months. I bought a well-worn but sturdy Wolseley car from Allen's father-in-law. It enabled us to take vacation trips to Adelaide, Canberra, and Sydney.

It never occurred to me at the outset of our Melbourne stay that we would make so many friends and that many of those relationships would continue for decades. Allen and his family came to upstate New York and he taught in my department at the community college in Troy. When both families were free, we enjoyed social and travel experiences together.

A few years after returning to Australia, Elizabeth died from melanoma at the age of sixty-two. Two years later, Allen married a fine lady named Pam who had a love of adventure and a great sense of humor.

We met up with the Hulls at Allen's daughter's home north of Calgary, Canada. From there we took a five-day driving tour of the Canadian Rockies. We borrowed his daughter's van. There was that occasion when we were ascending a lonely road up in the mountains to see a spectacular view which was every bit as beautiful as we were told.

Trouble ensued. In a remote parking lot, we returned to the van to find the keys were inside the locked vehicle. We tried every device we could think of to get a door open, but we had no luck. Allen found a log and was about to bash in the windshield when I discovered a very small vent window and broke it. Unfortunately, each of us was too big to reach in and undo the latch.

That's when a family with a very young child came out of the wooded area. "Can we borrow your youngster?" I asked. The boy was small enough to get his arm through the vent window. He undid the door lock.

What a relief to be on the road once again. Allen wanted to keep our *incident* a secret from his daughter and so we sneakily left the van to be repaired at a garage out of town, telling her that we took it in for an oil change.

The following day, the garage man phoned and the daughter answered. "We fixed that broken window in your van," he announced. Our cover was blown!

Following my retirement we visited Allen again in 1996, meeting up with he and Pam in Queesntown, New Zealand. Sandy passed away in 2005. I once again spent time in Melbourne in 2007.

Allen's birthday was December 31 and mine was a day later. Every year he would phone me on New Years' Eve to wish congratulations.

In 2010 I paid my last visit to Melbourne. I once again stayed with the Hulls. Grace was with me once again. I had originally planned to make the trip a year later in 2011, but for some reason went a year prior to what I had planned. Shortly after I left Melbourne, Allen suffered a debilitating stroke and was assigned to a rehab facility. He died a few years later.

JOE PODOBA

It was terrific to have a good friend as a neighbor. Joe moved next door to the homestead when he was only three, the youngest of a Czech immigrant family, who bought the Garrett Staats house, the only other residence on Staats Island. They were the hardest-working family I ever knew, toiling from dawn to dusk growing sweet corn in the warm weather months—starting out with plow horses and eventually using tractors.

The three Podoba children, Helen, Mary and Joe became our constant companions in the summer and on weekends in the cooler months (because we were off to Rensselaer for schooling during the week). As youngsters we were always involved in some type of physical activity—tag, croquet, swimming, exploring the river shore in the summer or sledding and tobog-ganing in the winter.

We grew up together through the teen years. In our late teens, Joe met up with a Rensselaer girl who was a friend of a friend of mine and so our relationship was maintained. His girl was great at playing popular music on the piano, and so there were frequent song-fests around the piano through our teen years.

Joe's folks ran the farm right up until his dad passed on unexpectedly at the early age of 53. It was anticipated that Joe would take over, since he had grown to be competent at just about every task that came his way. NOT! He had hated farming all his maturing years and couldn't wait to get on with his life, which included attending Syracuse University. Following college, the Army called—it was Korean War time and like so many of the rest of us, Joe went on active duty.

After the war, Joe met another young lady and they married in the 1950's with a memorable reception at the Crooked Lake Hotel. Joe took a job with the state which he maintained until retirement.

Over these 70+ years we have kept in contact. When I was doing a driving tour of the south in winter, I would spend a night or two with Joe and Sue at Myrtle Beach, where they moved to be near spiritually like-minded friends and to avoid the winter months. At the annual homestead Christmas party, they have made it a point to attend when they are visiting their children in the area. It's great that they enjoy it enough to bring along their children and grandchildren.

BOB HART

Bob Hart moved to Rensselaer from New York City in my junior year in high school. We became good buddies because he sat across the aisle from me in my home room. His arrival at the school was somewhat of a sensation because he was so extraordinarily good looking and liked to dance. The girls were enamored. Our mutual friendship developed because Bob enjoyed riding in and repairing my Model A ford and was particularly adept at electronics.

After high school Bob, like the rest of us, did a two year stint in the military assigned to a rolling and pitching Destroyer Escort (DE), a Navy ship noted for its discomfort. Returning to civilian life, he began his lifelong career as a repairman with the New York Telephone Company, an avenue of employment for those who preferred the out of doors and working with their hands. We kept in contact through social gatherings and he would frequently stop by the homestead where he could enjoy a favorite pastime of sailing on the Hudson River.

Bob married and had three children but the union didn't last because of his infidelity. The ladies were a distraction he couldn't resist. After his divorce, we maintained only infrequent contact.

After retirement, Bob found a partner and moved to Florida into a retirement campsite. His new partner had been a friend of mine since childhood and he couldn't have made a better choice. Together they developed the social life at the senior campsite as they became involved in community activities: opening a club house and pool, scheduling dances, dinners, theater productions and all around companionship get-togethers. Bob was always available at the campsite for helping neighbors with electrical problems. For me, their mobile home became a favorite stopover on my winter travels in the south. Their hospitality was most exemplary.

Incredibly, at the age of 77 Bob had an appendicitis attack and died within hours. Anne Kirsch, his partner, remains a close friend and we get together for lunch and social companionship whenever possible

WIL KOVELESKIE

How do you *inherit* a lifelong friend? For me it was a gradual process, taking years and years. Wil Koveleskie lived nearby in Rensselaer and was just a little younger than brother Barry, so it was natural that they would be drawn together through school and neighborhood activities. Wil was an only child and his single mom was an inveterate helicopter parent. Wil enjoyed being involved with our sizeable family. He appeared in our lives when he was eight years old and remained there as a permanent friend until his passing.

Wil was no barrel of excitement, but he was always a willing participant in any activities that came up. He was an ever-present companion at all games and physical activities such as swimming, boating, sledding, and tobogganing. He was always willing to lend a helping hand whenever work was required. At the homestead he was invaluable at pitching in with carpentry, mechanics, electrical assistance, etc.

He and brother Barry were inseparable companions through their teen years. They each did military service in World War II–Wil serving on active duty in the North Atlantic in the Armed Guard on merchant ships—and Barry stationed at a desk in Texas.

If there is one most memorable characteristic about Wil, it was his delight in needling his friends. Since Barry had a thin skin, Wil ceaselessly criticized him for sitting behind a desk while Wil was on the high seas. After the war ended, Barry and Wil returned home to civilian life. Wil took a menial job and Barry attended the local business college. They led the merry social life of bachelors, bar hopping and reveling into the wee hours. Barry found a terrific girl and Wil was then adrift for companionship. That's when he gravitated toward brother Larry and I—a relationship which developed over several decades.

I married in 1957. Since Wil got along extremely well with Sandy, our relationship continued. Wil was the kind of friend who was always available to lend a helping hand–literally. Once I got stuck in the snow at three a.m. in mid-winter and he readily came to my assistance.

Wil had a terrific sense of humor. For several of her years before retiring, Sandy did home care—usually with elderly people in their declining years. Often, however, she became attached to her patients and was always very sad when one of them passed on. She would dejectedly describe the loss with me and often with Wil present. On one occasion, Wil just shook his head and said: "Sandy please do me a favor. If I ever get sick, don't become my caretaker."

Wil married in the mid-60s and he selected a terrific partner. They had two children and have remained among our closest friends. One February day Rosemary and Wil stopped at the homestead for a visit. She and I were chatting when we heard a slight moan and a thud. Wil had collapsed and died instantly from heart failure with no previous indications that he was feeling under the weather. Wil was 77. His wife, Rosemary, remains a close friend.

Tom Hunt and Andy Miller

I link these two guys (and their wives) together because we had the commonality of being colleagues in the Business Division at Hudson Valley Community College for some 40 years. Our friendship grew over mutual respect. I was their teacher and Department Chairperson in the 70s. After being hired on years later as faculty Andy became one of the very best of accounting teachers—I learned that from conversations with his students.

Tom went on to become a most competent CPA, who not only developed a successful business in the town of Kinderhook (while teaching at HVCC fall semesters only), but also became active as a volunteer fireman and bank director. Tom and his wife Dee work side by side running the firm. They have been thoughtful friends, inviting me to social events. Until she passed away at 82, Tom looked after his Mom, inviting her to dinner on Sundays.

Andy and his wife, Pat, maintain a summer home on Sacandaga Lake and have an August get together there annually. Because of their continuing friendship, I feel truly blessed.

THE FALLONS

When Sandy and I arrived back from Australia in the summer of 1966, we were introduced to the newlyweds, the Fallons, who were at the time renting the north wing of the homestead— which we had occupied before going to Melbourne. We were able to move into a rental home in upper Rensselaer formerly occupied by Sandy's folks who were retiring to northern New York State.

Being with these new friends, Gretchen and Marty, was a little like having a blood transfusion—they emanated that spark and zest than only youth can provide. And, boy, did they take some adjusting to! Marty was a newly graduated social worker. Gretchen was involved in her dad's beauty supply distributorship.

They were as liberal as anyone with whom we had ever come in contact.

Marty was a great social worker, but initially he over-empathized with some of his clients, to the extent that he would temporarily share the occupancy of his home with needy families. Most of their friends were right in tune with the liberal philosophy of the '60s. Admittedly, some of those ideas rubbed off to us dyed-in-the-wool conservatives decades later.

The Fallons were truly enjoyable. Sometimes Gretchen's openness was amazing. She was a pack rat. If she needed something that she didn't have in their apartment, she would go to the older wing of the homestead, take whatever she needed—and always leave something in exchange. For example, if she was out of butter, she would *borrow* it from the homestead area, and leave in its place a pound of sugar. Sometimes it would become a challenge—I would see some fresh strawberries on the homestead kitchen table and then puzzle over what Gretchen may have borrowed in exchange for the fruit. We would always solve the mysteries as a result of subsequent conversations.

Gretchen would come out with the most outrageous conversation topics. I heard her talking to my *old-school* mother about the latest method of birth control she and Marty were using. My mother politely nodded, but I can just imagine her inner thoughts.

One time Gretchen asked Brother Larry whether he wore briefs or boxer shorts because she wanted to buy some for Marty. Larry admitted to wearing boxer shorts to which she innocently inquired, "but don't things *bang together* down there?" Unbelievable!

They both enjoyed being part of our extended family. Larry and Marty did a lot of sailing and outboard motor boating on the Hudson. Marty was always enthusiastic about pitching in to help with projects and he thoroughly enjoyed being with our young children and sharing doodlebug excursions with them and Uncle Larry.

Marty loved using the wood fireplace in their apartment. Trouble was, he would *borrow* my favorite chopping block and use it for fuel. I would be temporarily miffed, but there would always be another replacement block and, too, I really liked the guy.

They refer to their brief stay at the north wing of the apartment as the most precious years of their lives.

When brother Barry moved back to the area from New Jersey in 1968, he bought the north wing of the house from brother Kim and, as a result, Marty and Gretchen had to move out. They chose to return to their home town area near Rochester, NY. Later they bought a condo in Naples, FL.

It has been several decades since the Fallons moved, but we continue to maintain close contact. They have two terrific daughters who also remain friends. We have attended their family celebrations and they have come to ours. They have always managed to visit when in the area.

THE AKLANDS

In the late '60s a young newly-wedded couple, Bob and Carolyn Akland, joined the First Church in Albany. They immediately became involved in church affairs, including governance and Christian education. Bob Alkand and I were among the younger officers and we soon realized that we would be acting as a team when it came to the Board of Trustees policy decisions. His wife, Carolyn was active in youth education. In the early '70s, Bob talked me into joining the choir. Thence began our social connection in addition to church governance activities. The choir director initiated social outings and, too, I began inviting the Aklands to our extended-family functions.

Dr. Jim Van Hoeven was our Senior Pastor for several years. He was an excellent preacher-but for some reason disliked by several members of the governing boards. His suggestion to have an elevator installed in our seven-leveled building was roundly rejected on the basis of cost. Bob and I worked vigorously in favor of the minister's plan, but there was overwhelming resistance from a few influential members of the Board of Trustees.

Once again grace was on our side. A few years after the elevator presentation was tabled, a wealthy widow passed on, leaving the church approximately

$1 million. Now there could no longer be any strong opposition to the elevator on the basis of cost. It was Bob Akland who supervised the many details involved in the elevator installation—as well as several other renovation changes. Since we have an aging congregation, the elevator has proved to be a godsend. -

Several years ago, Bob and Carolyn Akland acquired a lovely old farmhouse far from the church and have transferred their membership to a small church near their rural homestead. We make it a point to get together for brunch at least once a year. Even though they live far from the church, they thoughtfully look after aging members of our congregation. They have children and grandchildren, which even more reinforces our friendship through commonality.

THE BURNS

Jean Greenshields was a neighbor in the lower end of Rensselaer when I was in elementary school. She met Jim Burns, whom she tutored in English while in high school. Jim was a returning WWII vet who had dropped out of school to join the Navy. After several years of courtship, they married.

I went to the teacher's college with Jean and she took a reading-related English teaching job.

Jim went into management at the local utility firm. He developed a friendship with brother Larry and so we always were in contact. Both Jim and Jean have remained very active in the Loudonville Community Church in nearby Latham. Jim has also been most involved with Camp Pinnacle in the Heldeberghs, a Christian retreat and summer camp.

Our paths have crossed and re-crossed through mutual friendships and social activities over the years. They attended our first Christmas carol sing some 60 years ago and have seldom missed one since. The have a son and two grandsons living in Colorado. It is always a treat to have Jim and Jean drop by at the homestead for a few hours of *catching-up* conversation. It is also reassuring to me to have friends who are even older than I. They are interesting friends because they have traveled, they read, and they remain active. Jim even went sail parasailing when in his 80s!

I have been truly blessed with so many long term close friendships.

JANIE AND THE JONES'

In more recent decades, additional friends have joined the extended family. Janie Gerwin worked with sister-in-law Torill in the Rensselaer school system and re-tired at about the same time. Her love of family, travel and community events makes for interesting companionship. Her cooking is legendary.

David and Maggie Jones became friends of Brother Larry through the Singles' Ski

Club back in the late 20th century. They, too, get out and go—enjoying skiing, Hudson River swimming, travel and family relationships. And, too, Maggie is a great cook.

When there is work to be done at the homestead, count on help from Janie and the Jones'.

The culinary connection becomes particularly valuable as we gather weekly on Sundays to enjoy a group dinner. There are 7 or 8 different contributing families who take turns by supplying the main course, and E-mailing the other prospective attendants for additional dishes. It works out very well with a schedule set out 3 months in advance on a distributed calendar.

Enjoying appetizers, liquid refreshments and stimulating conversation at the riverside gazebo, on the veranda, or at the living room fireside is something to look forward to.

ANDREWS AND GILBERT

This listing wouldn't be complete without including Dick Andrews and Don Gilbert, colleagues with whom I shared chairperson responsibilities for decades at Hudson Valley Community College. Ours was the ideal job—classroom teaching, advising students, guiding faculty. working with support staff, along with considerable academic administration.

There were challenges but overall it was an enjoyable experience. The chairpersons had our own organization and through that I became friends with Dick Andrews, head of physical science, and Don Gilbert, chairperson of Criminal Justice. Couple those academic areas with my Accounting specialization and that covered a disparate range. As usual, the binding ingredient was humor and we had a lot of it through dealing with every level from the President of the college to the students. Most of my chairperson colleagues subscribed to the conviction that the students were the most important of all levels.

Dick and Don and I got to enjoy each other's company so much that it spilled over to social occasions off the campus–lunches and conferences with other chairs further enriched out relationship. We even invited each other and spouses to extended family social occasions. After retirement our friendship has continued through enjoyable get-togethers where we keep up with personal and external developments. More grace to be sure.

Six

Education / Career / Travel

Elementary School

It's amazing to me that memories can be retained for so many decades, and that I have stored so many recollections of my school and college years, which, incidentally took place within 15 miles of my home: grade one through graduate courses.

Fond recollections of the elementary school include:

I was with my family when we came across my second grade teacher, Miss Farnam, and her friends who had also been walking in Thatcher Park, a popular regional attraction. I think it was then that I first realized that teachers were human beings, too! I had only seen teachers in the classroom and had no idea that they had a life outside of class. This one enjoyed walking–which meant she might even also enjoy listening to the radio, doing dishes, petting a dog, etc. Maybe even she used the toilet! What a revelation!

In November of the third grade, I was burned severely and had to spend four months in the hospital. Incredibly, my third grade teacher, Miss Holmes, showed up faithfully at the hospital every Wednesday to be with me during visiting hours!

In the fourth grade, I recall classmate Joan Cummings and the rest of us cautiously dipping our straight pens into our inkwells when practicing penmanship. Mishap occurred. Joan spilled some ink onto her dress and she began to cry. Then her fingers became covered with spilled ink and she cried some more. And then to stop the flow of tears she rubbed her eyes with her fingers which turned the entire eye-socket area dark blue. Seeing this, the class went into gales of laughter which made Joan cry and rub her

eyes even more. I don't recall how the teacher resolved the crisis, but eventually Joan was calmed
and allowed to go home.

Aunt Bess strictly forbid us to use the lavatory
at school. "I do not want you to catch diseases
spread by other children," she admonished us.
She gave her consent to using the urinal, but
never, ever, the toilet seat. It instilled fear of social diseases in me forever onward.

Miss Clara Rich, the fifth grade teacher, was a
feared disciplinarian. There were two fifth grade
classes and I so hoped I would be channeled in
with the friendlier teacher. Oh no, I drew the
dreaded card–Miss Rich–and boy did I toe the
line at that awkward stage of life when hormones
dominate our actions, making us silly, unruly
and out of control. Interestingly, Miss Ross liked
me and I think that in our year together, she
even smiled at me once or twice.

Another feared teacher, specializing in English,
was a strict, no-nonsense crab and once again,
I was gripped with dread. Miss McMcann, was a
short, 60ish, heavy-set, grouchy looking spinster
with her hair tied in a bun and horned rimmed
glasses mounted on her nose. She could humble

her charges with just a glare, and she did it effectively for the two years (seventh and eighth grade) we had her for our English classes.

Miss McCann would say things that, in today's classroom atmosphere, would have cost her job. For instance, when someone got out of hand she once shrieked, "What's the matter with your parents–you just weren't brought up right!" Or the time a Jewish student failed to hand in an assignment. "You miss your class obligations, but you never miss YOUR HOLIDAYS!" she shouted.

And I couldn't get over the Evans girl when she summoned the nerve to reply to Miss McCann after being chastised as lazy: "You know, Miss McCann, that all work and no play makes Jack a dull boy." That impertinent remark caused Miss McCann eyes to bulge and her face to turn blue with anger as she screamed back poetically, "And all play and no work makes Jack want to shirk." This heated exchange brought the classroom to a dead calm.

But there was a flip side to that feared lady. She taught us proper grammar whether we liked it or not. She did it with repetition and I can still hear such guidance joggers as "I' before 'e' except after 'c' when pondering how to spell 'receive'" or "there's 'a rat' in separate" or "stationery is spelled with an 'e' when referring to paper. That other spelling, 'stationary' refers to standing still." It was clever and it worked.

At rest time, we would put our heads down on our folded arms for 15 minutes. After that she read to us with awe and enthusiasm which made the literature come alive. She chose, *The Wonderful One-Horse Shay* about the deacon's carriage which lasted exactly 100 years to the day, and *The Revolt of Mother* about the fed-up farm wife who was so sick of her farmer husband's devotion to his barn that she moved all of the household belongings into it. She also read *Silas Marner* and *The Merchant of Venice*. And she read us poetry, which included *Trees* by Joyce Kilmer, most of which I can recite to this day.

At the offset, I dreaded being assigned to Miss McCann's homeroom. By the time I graduated from the eighth grade, I was convinced that she had to be one of my most respected and competent teachers of all time. How proud she was when I stood up at graduation to receive the second highest grade point award for English (damned that classmate, Lois Bissell, for coming in first.

I also remember my first loves in those grammar school years. The hormones raged to the point I would get uncontrollable *stiffies* at my desk and dreaded to stand and recite with this *tent* poking out into my trousers. I fell in love with Gerry and she wasn't even pretty. And I fell in love with Alice and even knitted her a belt. I also fell in love with Norma because she was developing *bumps* on her upper torso.

Secondary School

Our grammar school experience ended with the eighth grade. Following that it was off to the high school at the north end of the city. There we combined with the three other grade feeder schools. It was a whole new life experience including riding the school bus, eating in a cafeteria, learning locker combinations, etc. At the age of 15 it all seemed overwhelming. There was also the adjustment to a different home room teacher, regular changes of class, and new classmates.

I find it a source of pride that a few of the classmates I met in home room were to become friends for the rest of my life.

The Freshmen Reception was intimidating. The boys gathered on one side of the gym and the girls on the other. Between us stretched the dance floor. We had only been at the high school for a few weeks so the hormones hadn't kicked in enough for couples to form. It was a bold move to ask a girl to dance. I had my eye on a potential partner, but when I popped the question she turned me down flat. I took notice, however, that she later danced with someone else, which I considered to be rude.

Apparently my destiny that night was to be a hero. One girl, who wasn't very attractive, had been shunned and was crying because of that. Out of nowhere my home room teacher appeared at my side. "Staats," she said "I want you to go over there and dance with Margie. She's crying her eyes out because no one will ask her to dance, and I've noticed that you are a good dancer." I followed her suggestion. She was an excellent dance partner. Out of the corner of my eye I could see a few of my buddies snickering at me but, you know what? It felt good to come to the rescue of a damsel in distress.

By the sophomore year, friendships had begun to gel. We didn't think about it at the time, but the college entrance/jocks/cheerleader crowd were resented because of our being in a clique. As I look back, that exclusivity was thoughtless and unkind, but I understand it is still going on.

The social whirl began with a picnic at a regional state park. About a dozen or so of us seemed to hit it off and so it remained for the next three years. We would meet at each other's houses for popcorn, soda, and games. One classmate's home became our favored hangout because the parents were so hospitable and enjoyed the youth and enthusiasm of their daughter's friends.

A buddy of mine had a clubhouse in his back yard where we would spend Saturday mornings listening to the 10 top tunes on the radio. We attended all of the basketball games, since several of the friends were jocks and cheerleaders. There was a local candy store where we spent lots of fun time. I don't think the proprietor made much money, but he enjoyed our group of teenagers.

My love life was, in a word, uncertain. I had such a fear of rejection that I simply didn't have the courage to ask someone for a date.

I recall an interesting conversation with my favorite math teacher regarding a Jewish girl with whom I had begun to spend time. This day and age the teacher probably would have been fired for what she said, but things were different back then. The teachers acted as our guardians and often hovered over us like parents. All of the faculty knew that my mom was a widow and had endured a tough life, so they were on the lookout to see after my five siblings and me. I was the last of the lot and had done well academically. I was not at the top of the class, but was consistently within the top 10 percent.

When my friendship with the young girl of a different faith accelerated, I was taken aside. "You know, Staats, it's probably not a good idea for you to be seeing Barbara," my teacher advised. "Your faiths are worlds apart and that could spell a very rocky future." As I got to know the young lady better, I realized that the math teacher was right. She was a fun partner, particularly talented on the piano, but her family situation was just too different from mine. We remained friends, however, for some 50 years.

Before graduating from high school, I repaid this fantastic math teacher in an unusual way academically. Toward the end of the year, those of us in the academic program took New York State Regents' exams in several different subjects. In my senior year my math regents was trigonometry. I studied so hard that I slept far into the morning, well after the exam had begun. I was awakened by a phone call. It was Miss Womer, the math teacher. "Staats, where are you?" she asked. I couldn't believe that I'd overslept. "I'll be there as soon as possible," I responded, bounding from my bed and into my clothes and onto the bus headed for school. Breathless.

When I arrived at the school, Miss Womer met me at the door. "Calm down and have some milk and a sandwich," she smiled, offering me something she had bought to fill my empty stomach. I started the exam an hour later than the others and my grade amazed both

Miss Wormer and I–99! Amazing. She could have let me dangle in the wind by attending summer school, but she cared enough to contact me.

College(s)

Our family never had much money. Attending a private college was out of the question, although I had been accepted at the US Coast Guard Academy in New London, CT, based on my score in a nationwide exam. My choices were to secure a scholarship or to attend the local State Teacher's College which had a whopping $42 per semester tuition.

By living at home and taking a part time job, the door was open for me to study for the teaching profession. Attending the New York State College for Teachers in Albany proved to be one of my wisest decisions because, once in the profession, I loved every minute of it.

I made a couple of detours, however. After the first year at the state college I once again was accepted at the Coast Guard Academy and off I went. In the first week, however, I realized that I'd made a big mistake. I was homesick, having found a new sweetheart, and didn't enjoy the military atmosphere of the academy. We had to get up at five in the morning and row in sculls out on the Thames River. "Flutter your oars, Staats," came the command from the coxswain and I had no idea what I was doing wrong.

"On the drill field for extra marching practice, Staats," came another command to pathetic me who always had trouble differentiating my left from my right. Crazy! Not only that, I learned that one of the main functions of the Coast Guard at the time was to patrol the North Atlantic for icebergs! Not me. And to top it all off, I was having trouble getting to sleep because of the frequent motion going on when my upper-bunk roommate masturbated night after night.

I dropped out and was able to get back to classes at the teachers' college and complete my second year. College was fun but I'd had 14 years of education in a row. There were the usual proms and beer parties but I needed a change. Thence, I spent two years on active duty with the Navy.

The two-year active duty break with the military must have matured me because my grades after renewing college soared to Dean's list following the mediocre first two years. I was definitely more focused. I appreciated my professors more, but still managed to pick some doozies. One math professor was so bright that he would write a formula on the board with his right hand and immediately apply the eraser with his left hand. "This is as easy as falling off Robin Hood's barn," he uttered repeatedly–whatever that meant.

For Integral Calculus, I sat in a class run by the head of the Math Department, who had the peculiar habit of looking over our heads. He seemed totally out of touch with those of us who were struggling. And so I struggled no more, fleeing from math major to business education major. There I was on enjoyable turf and the road ahead became less stressful.

Still, there were unique professors. One memorable philosophy professor had a droll dry wit. The way he took attendance was to hand out a sheet of paper containing a grid of empty boxes. The grid represented our classroom seating plan. We were to write our name in the box representing our position on the grid. I was feeling devilish one Good Friday morning and signed *Mamie Eisenhower* in my box. Eventually, the professor scanned the sign sheet and commented, "Even though it's only nine in the morning, it's been an eventful day. In this class I have Mamie Eisenhower, and in my earlier class I was graced with the presence of Judas Iscariot." The class broke into a roar.

Post-Graduate Programs

In 1956 I earned a BS in Business Education and decided to stay on one more year for my Master's. By this time I'd met the love of my life, and we were married late in June in 1957 the day before my graduation ceremony. Staying on for the graduate degree immediately after getting the BS was a wise decision. I saved a year of formal study, because in the future the Master's degree term was lengthened to two years. More importantly, I would have had to take advanced courses part time, and with seven children in my future, that could have been a strain.

After the respite of a year or two, however, it was time to move on with more formal education with the goal of eventually earning a doctor's degree. I was teaching in Hudson High School at the time, when a colleague urged me to join him in taking weekend courses at a college some distance from home, the University of Connecticut (UConn) in the village of Storrs. This required driving some 80 miles on a Friday night and taking one course Friday evening and another on Saturday morning before driving back home. I only put up with that routine for two semesters, but my fellow teacher pursued it to the end.

As usual there were some unique experiences associated with UConn. One time I let my wit get away with me, and I believe it cost me a letter grade. The *A* I was earning in Psychology was dropped to a *B* and it was all my fault. Professor Wilkes had to be the dullest teacher alive at the time. To slog through a monotonous class after a week of teaching and the lengthy drive to UConn was a challenging experience. And so I was ready to enliven the class when the good professor made an inquiry: "Mr. Staats, what inspires you to drive all that distance just to take this course?" The class shared my opinion that the professor was an agonizingly dull, so laughter erupted when I responded, "I come all this distance because I learned that you were teaching this class!" Goodbye *A*, hello *B*.

Concurrently, I ran into a stroke of luck which I think moved my *B* to an *A*. The Saturday morning class was conducted by Harvey Fuller, the Superintendent of Schools in the city of Wethersfield, CT. He was enthusiastic, fun, and full of practical information. I would rave about him around home. My Mom brought to my attention that we had relatives living in Wethersfield that we hadn't seen in years. "Ask Mr. Fuller if somehow or another he might know the Bowmans," she suggested. When I mentioned the name Bowman to Professor Fuller, his face lighted up. "You happen to be asking about the closest friend I've had for decades," he responded. I'm sure that this influenced his grading decision. Goodbye *B*, hello *A*. Not only did he give me a top grade, but he arranged a luncheon meeting inviting my mom, my wife and me and also the Bowmans. Later on, they came to the homestead for an afternoon of renewed friendship.

After a year of traveling to UConn, the novelty wore off and I enrolled locally at the Graduate School of

Public Affairs, sponsored by Syracuse University. One after another, each course became a continuously boring slog fest because the content was geared toward state government workers. Dull text material about bureaucracy was difficult to get though, because so much of the content seemed mundane and common sense. And the jargon was obfuscated and unnecessarily repetitive.

For several years, I returned to the graduate program and when it came to the comprehensive finals, I realized I'd made a monumental mistake. I had stretched my education over too many years. The professors who set the finals were not the ones I had in class because there had been so much faculty turnover. Hence, the questions posed were from a different point of view that those I'd learned from an earlier faculty member. When I received notice that I had failed the comprehensives, it was a devastating blow. I'd taken at least 60 credits of postgraduate work and didn't earn the doctor's degree I worked so hard to get. For several months, I was in a funk.

That is when faith came in. My spirituality lifted me out of depression and into a much more optimistic frame of mind. True, I had not succeeded at the graduate program, but far more important was the fact that I had a terrific family, a job I loved, friends galore, and so much other support to fall back on. Life goes on.

Forays Into Part Time Work

There had been a variety of jobs in my teen years, but none of them lasted long.

My first pay was earned selling scrap iron with my older brother, Kim. Old Port of Albany docks along the Hudson had been disassembled and the Staats family had agreed to let the construction company dump their discarded wood on our river shore. The docks had been held together by heavy duty iron bars which could easily be removed from the wooden dock materials.

For a few months, we carted the scrap iron to the local buyer and the cash seemed to flow–sometimes a whopping $60 a week! I remember what I did with my first wad of cash–I bought a purple satin long-sleeved shirt that I thought was the last word in fashion wear. It sure was an attention getter! One time, I proudly wore the shirt and white pants to a classy eatery in Albany. Let me tell you–eyes turned. I thought it was out of admiration until another customer tapped me on the shoulder and asked, "Just out of curiosity, are you a jockey at Saratoga Race Track?" That took me back a few pegs and the damned shirt was relegated to my closet forevermore.

My second paycheck went toward a combination ra-dio/record player. TV hadn't yet made an appearance commercially. And then on to the purchase of every record the Andrews Sisters had made at the time. For me it was paradise listening.

My only other job before going into the Navy was as a part-time filing clerk with an insurance company in downtown Albany. The pay was minimal and the job was boring, but I worked with dozens of older women, all of whom seemed to have an amazing sense of humor. As the only young guy in the crowd, I was the darling, receiving my share of edible goodies, naughty jokes, and general horse play.

The ladies decided to take me to dinner once they found out I was leaving for the Navy. The goodbye party took place at Kapp's in the Hollow, Rensselaer's finest restaurant. The ladies insisted I have a whiskey sour–and several more. I think I was treated to a steak dinner, but it was all a very hazy evening after the alcohol began to flow.

The only thing that pulled me out of my inebriated state was the harsh rebuke I received from my mother who was a teetotaler to the nth degree. It just so happened that, at the time, I'd been reading a best seller titled *Mrs. Mike,* a woman who'd married a Royal Mounted Policeman and moved to the Canadian wilderness where she worked among the Eskimos battling diphtheria–a fatal disease resulting in throwing up volumes of blood before dying. When I arrived home at the wee hours, I staggered into the bathroom and knelt before the toilet bowl, proceeding to vomit profusely. The spew was speckled with bits of red which was caused by the many maraschino cherries in the whiskey sours, of course. In my misery I was sure the bits of cherry were blood and that I, too, was dying of diphtheria.

"Mom." I cried out, "I think I'm dying from diphtheria." To which she coldly responded "Then I hope you die." No sympathy there so I crawled into my bedroom and just about died.

The teaching profession gave me summers free. With a young family, idling the time away wasn't an option. During the first two years, I took a summer job delivering mail on foot for the Rensselaer Post Office, taking over for those on vacation.

I had a personal friend, Archie, a few years older than I who had taken a postman's job immediately after high school graduation. I replaced him for two weeks. What an experience! I soon found that Archie had a unique routine. At the time Rensselaer had more than a dozen bar rooms. At each one on Archie's delivery route, I encountered a friendly bartender with two freshly poured beers awaiting my arrival–all of this starting at about eleven in the morning. In the first two or three days on the job by mid-afternoon I was staggering from house to house. I soon realized that drinking on the job was a very poor idea.

A few days after his return, Archie approached me in the post office with this message: "You owe me a kiss–for f-cking me over with some of my customers while I was away. They tell me you either put it in the wrong place or forgot it entirely." I apologized.

Sadly, in his early forties, Archie died from alcoholism.

Dogs were a problem along the mail route. It seemed to me that the smaller snappier ones were among those to be most wary although a couple of brutes were also intimidating. My scariest experience was with a cocker spaniel which seemed to be sleeping peacefully on the landing of a steep outside staircase leading to the second story mailbox. I noticed that, although he seemed to be sleeping, he actually had one eye half opened and focused on me. Just as I dropped the letters in the box, he suddenly leaped to his feet and bit my leg. This was in the days before mace became a defense mechanism.

And then there was the time I got caught up in a late week-night celebration with a good friend who lived next door to the homestead. He and I had each become the father of a son within days of each other. He stopped by for a dust cutter and then we had another. And so on. Daylight came about before we called it quits. I had to be at the post office by 7 a.m. on a sweltering hot day. What a day to be delivering mail!

On my route, I drove the mail truck to a suburban neighborhood where I loaded my shoulder bag and left the truck to deliver the mail on foot. In my condition,

I plodded along, footstep after footstep–counting the hours until quitting time. At one stop, I came to an apartment complex for which a key was required to open the boxes. That same key was on the ring which held the key to the mail truck–which was my downfall since I left the key in one of the boxes and didn't discover the loss until I returned to the truck. And of course, I had no idea as to the whereabouts of the missing key.

With considerable trepidation, I phoned the post office to report the dilemma of the missing mailbox truck key. Upon hearing my pathetic story he said unsympathetically, "Staats, you do realize that losing the key to a US Mail truck is a federal offense." And then he let me hang there for a long pause until he continued, "However, in your case, we'll send someone out with a replacement key. Stay where you are." As if I had a choice. I was greatly relieved later on in the day when one of the apartment dwellers discovered the keys and phoned the post office.

Teaching

One of the most important choices I ever made was not a deliberate one. After secondary school I only had enough money to attend the local state teachers' college. The tuition was a mere $42 a semester! I think I was more interested in something more exciting, like acting or work in the media–but I became certified as a teacher and at the time the job market was wide open, even though the pay was not lucrative.

During forty-seven years, I advanced from practice teaching, to high school teaching, to college teaching and for the final seven years I taught as an adjunct.

Knowing when to quit was a decision which came about suddenly and with few qualms. As an adjunct my subject was a generalized computer software course which gave the students a few weeks of experience in the areas of word processing, spread sheeting, data base and power point. It was a very practical late-afternoon course, particularly for those older adults who approached computer use with trepidation. The only problem is that traditionally-aged college students in their late teens and early twenties flooded the classrooms simply to get credit and that most of those young people had already gained computer experience over several years of their lives and, quite frankly, were sometimes more proficient in certain areas than I was.

My day of reckoning came as a new semester opened. I was showing the students how to record and copy data onto the 2" square floppy disks which we were using at the time.

I have to give the young man credit for being diplomatic–he waited until the class was over and the classroom was clear.

"Professor Staats," he politely addressed me. "For some time many of us have been using these to record data." He handed me a flash drive, also known as a thumb drive because of its compact design. I had never before seen one. Then and there I decided it was time to move on to retirement and within days I informed my dean of the decision to wind it up at the end of the semester. For several years I had adjusted over and over again to changes in hardware as well as software and it was time to get off the train. I never regretted the decision to quit.

Travel

The urge to travel began in the seventh grade when we studied geography—I enjoyed it thoroughly. My travel experience was extremely limited, however, until I joined the Navy at the age of 20. In addition to basic training in the state of Maryland, I got to spend time in Puerto Rico and in the Canadian Maritime States of Nova Scotia, New Brunswick, and Newfoundland.

On our honeymoon Sandy and I visited all of the New England states and from then on it became a quest to see as much of the rest of the world as possible.

We traveled in every state in the union and over a period of 45 years took photos all 50 state capitols—including a second state capitol erected in Hawaii.

In Europe we visited Austria, Holland, Belgium, Portugal, Greece, Italy, Germany, Switzerland, Norway, Sweden, Denmark, France, Luxemburg, England and Iceland. In Africa my sons and I spent a few days in Egypt. In South America, Sandy and I explored Brazil, Uruguay, Argentina, Bolivia and Peru. We loved Australia and New Zealand and Tahiti. I visited several nations in Asia including Thailand, Singapore, Indonesia, Sri Lanka, Cambodia and India.

There are other destinations I would like to have visited but at this stage of life, long distance travel has lost its appeal. Given the chance, I would also like to have gone to the Baltics, the Greek Islands, South Africa, and the Caribbean. Nevertheless, the substantial travel I enjoyed has provided an endless supply of memories for which I am grateful.

Money is often cited as a reason for not traveling. If spending money I didn't have prevented me from traveling, I would never have accumulated the wealth of memories which are now a major source of comfort in my golden years. The sights seen, the friendships made, the exhilaration of time spent traveling with loved ones, particularly my wife, are indelible memories.

My first expensive journey was to spend a year in Australia. In order to do that I borrowed from friends to supplement my limited savings. It was all paid back with moderate interest.

Over the years I set aside a separate travel fund which I tapped when taking a trip. I often overspent the account, but never regretted it. Having a bundle in savings could never be more satisfying than having the experience of seeing the USA and so many other world sights–and spending time with so many hospitable people.

Seven

PHYSICAL ACCOMPLISHMENTS

C ould a lifetime of physical exercise and accomplishments relate in any way to my sudden psychological
adjustments to reaching the age of 83? The answer is
that extreme frustration arose as a result of inability to
function as in earlier years. As a youth growing up in the
country, there were always chores to be done and some
of them were physically challenging. Water had to be carried several hundred feet from the well to the house. The
vegetable garden had to be tended. Chopping wood was
a never-ending chore. Cutting grass with a reel-style hand
mower wasn't much fun but it sure was good exercise.

Homestead Projects

When World War II came to an end, my older brothers returned home from military service. Eldest brothers Larry and Kim proceeded to approach the other cousins owning the homestead to see if they would be willing to sell their ownership rights. As my dad's widow, my mother already owned one fourth of the estate. Cousin Jenn (Mrs. Phillip) Staats signed over her share for a pittance. Cousin Betty (Mrs. Jack Schell) negotiated and a compromise was reached. Aunt Mabel's one-fourth share had to be acquired from the city of Newburgh since she died intestate as a ward of that institution. At this point, brothers Larry and Kim each acquired half of an interest in Hoogebergh. They reached an agreement whereby Kim would fully own and occupy the north wing of the homestead and that Larry would divide his share equally among his siblings and mother and have ownership of the old fieldstone section of the house.

By the end of World War II, the homestead was in a very dilapidated state and desperately needed every sort of renovation involving carpentry, plumbing, electricity, masonry, etc. We had the manpower but not the money. Several of us had the energy, time, and interest and for the next 60 years an amazing amount of improvements to the homestead took place. It seems that brothers Larry and Barry as well as myself always had a project going. Many of these endeavors required pooling our energy while others became solo accomplishments.

Kitchen Fireplace (Brother Larry)

My earliest recollection of a most serious commitment of time and effort was when Brother Larry tackled the renovation of the upstairs bedroom fireplace which included completely rebuilding the fireplace and chimney which served the kitchen on the first floor. This required removing a wooden wall from the upstairs bedroom. It is just short of miraculous that the house hadn't caught fire decades earlier. Unknown to the occupants because the wooden wall covering remained in place, the bricks in the flue had disintegrated and fallen down at the base of the fireplace. When Larry took off the wooden covering, he saw that the protective layer of bricks had crumbled and fallen into a heap and that the wood was badly charred on the inside.

Larry removed all of the disintegrated bricks and rebuilt the arch supporting the chimney in the kitchen below. It was laborious and it was done with precision. Once the arch in the kitchen was in place, Larry took his time replacing the old bricks with new to build a flue which led from the kitchen up two stories through the roof with three feet of brick chimney capping the east end of the roof. The project took several months and was a virtual solo accomplishment.

While Larry was a diligent worker at home he had to take time to go to sea and earn enough to support himself.

THE NORTH WALL (BROTHER LARRY)

Years later, Larry pursued another masonry project. Over the centuries, the fieldstone wall at the northeast section of the house had developed leaks through the gradual erosion of mortar. Eventually the situation became so aggravated that a person could feel the wind whistling though the stonework on blustery winter days. The work required replacing the mortar in the supporting wall. This took months and months of patient rebuilding, but surely it added to the life of the structure.

REPLACING MORTAR ON THE SOUTH AND EAST WALLS (ME)

It's interesting how a seemingly uncomplicated project can grow into a major undertaking. During the late 1950's it caught my attention that there was loose mortar between most of the exterior wall fieldstones at the homestead which was eroding and that there were gaping empty spaces remaining. At first, I would get a bucket of water and mix up a batch of cement and take care of a small area which needed new mortar. As the work progressed, it became obvious that the entire southern and eastern outside walls were in dire need of refurbishing, mainly in the form of replacing eroded mortar.

For six summers, I devoted myself to the job which involved significant effort, particularly in climbing up and down a ladder. It was early on in my teaching career and I had the summers free. What better way to spend time than to work two or three hours each morning puttering with sand and cement. It was slow going, but a desperately needed task. In later years as my children came along, I had to find summer employment, but for the present I was contented with working on the homestead

And, oh, did I get advice. Because of its location at the end of a country road, the homestead seemed to attract those souls who simply get behind the steering wheel and point the car in whatever direction–which often turned out to be the front yard of the homestead. But how did so many of these old guys become experts in re-mortaring seventeenth century houses I often wondered.

I would be working away contentedly when thoughts were interrupted by the closing of a car door. In no time at all a shadow would appear at the foot of the ladder.

"What are you doing?" came the inquiry.

I'm replacing the mortar holding the fieldstones in place. Sure looks like it's needed, doesn't it?" I'd respond in a friendly way.

"Are you sure you have the mixture right?" came the inevitable question.

"I'm using two parts cement and one part sand. It seems to be working just fine." Often the old guy would shake his head in disagreement. "Doesn't seem right to me," he venture. Should be more like three parts sand and one of cement." I'm sure he was placing an educated guess.

"Well, this is what I've been told to use by stone masons and I'm sticking with it," I said with authority laced in a condescending tone. It usually had the desired effect–the departure of the curious onlooker.

Over the years, I have wondered about whether or not the mix was right, but some 60 years have passed and the mortar is still holding up. Maybe I was just lucky!!

Outbuildings (Larry and I)

Up until the 1950s, the outbuildings on the premises had consisted of an outhouse and a barn which my Mom burned to the ground one spring afternoon while several of us decided to take a lengthy walk to enjoy the spring. The dried grass from the past fall provided fine tinder for our aging arsonist. Unfortunately, the dried grass wasn't far from the barn, a structure which had just about reached the last stage of disintegration and was about to collapse.

From a mile or so away, our walking group could see smoke rising from the area of the homestead. Sure enough, Mom had set the grass alight–and then of course the winds came up and sent the fire sweeping toward the barn. We hastened back home, making way for incoming fire trucks, ambulances, etc. Surely enough, Mom had done a thorough job of burning the barn to the ground. Inside the barn had been stored a perfectly good diving board and a Model A Ford utility vehicle which had already been stripped down almost to the frame. Now it was simply a twisted remnant of its former self.

With the loss of the barn, the only storage area left was the homestead itself and within a few years, it became very cluttered. Where do you store a canoe in winter? In the upstairs hall of course. How about the veranda furniture which graces the front porch in summertime–in the downstairs hallway. Vehicles and mowers and such?–out in the weather.

Something had to be done. Brother Larry provided the idea, much of the manpower, and what cash was needed to build a sturdy boatshed a few hundred feet south of the homestead. Much of the structural material came from timbers which became available when the nearby Port of Albany replaced its aging wooden docks with metal structures.

The boatshed, completed in 1972, provided room to store a few small boats–canoes, rowboats and kayaks and a shelter for two vehicles. In addition there was a fine workshop area where tools and electrical equipment would be available.

As the years passed, the need for additional storage space expanded. In the mid 1980s, there was no room to store lawn tractors or other vehicles on the premises during the harsh northeast winters.

That gave me the idea to build a pole barn. The stall was only 8 feet wide and it stood about 10 feet high at the entrance and 20 feet deep, and sloped down to 8 feet. It was a simple structure using indigenous black locust trees as the vertical stanchions and rough cut lumber from a nearby sawmill for the roof supports. A 5/8" plywood covering was protected by sheets of stainless steel roofing. The next year, a second pole barn was built abutting the first one. Then ambition really kicked in and two wider 10' stalls were added. Eventually walls were added and a cement floor was poured in the two larger stalls, making the structure fit to be used as a garage for conducting repair work.

Brother Larry used his considerable skills to put in shelving and electrical outlets. In subsequent years, a separate multi-stall pole barn was built for boat storage. Of course that, too, has also filled up.

THE COMPOST TOILET (ME)

The homestead has never had an indoor toilet. Perhaps sometime in the future? In the meantime family and guests have to brave the elements (and the aroma) to get physical relief. As long as I can recall, which would mean going back to the 1930s, there has been a lone outhouse a hundred feet from the kitchen door. My mother used to kill the odor with a product called Chlorinated Lime and it did its job to an extent. Of course, the younger male members of the family and their friends deviously sought other locations to find relief.

As described, during the latter half of the 20th century, the family hosted countless parties, including sumptuous dinners, weddings, birthday celebrations, etc. To provide for such festive occasions, it has often been a policy to rent one or two Port-a-Johns. While pricey, they added sanitary facilities located near the action.

Nevertheless, the absence of a lavatory has been a drawback over the years.

In the 1980's a second outdoor toilet was built down by the boatshed. That provided some relief and more convenience since it was at the lower level of the property and considerably more accessible than the older john near the house.

In the early 1990s, I decided to construct a compost toilet. It would be close to the house and would not only be aroma-free, but would also not need any water for flushing. Just build a shed, install a toilet bowl and order from a Massachusette firm an underground tank resembling an iron lung to store the waste, and add peat moss after using the facility. It took a month to build the shed and dig a hole large enough for the tank (placed under the shed) to hold the waste. The shed was constructed near the boatshed because that's where the tools were available. It was built on a sled which, when the building was completed, was dragged by tractor up to its current location. The dimensions were 8 feet long and 6 feet wide and about 8 feet high. Only half of the interior was needed for the toilet room–the other half would be used as a dual-purpose storage room and clothes changing facility for bathers.

Unfortunately, the compost toilet doesn't take care of itself. The holding tank has to be rotated on a regular basis to allow the contents to bake into what looks somewhat like tobacco ash. There is no odor because a handful of peat moss is tossed into the toilet bowl after each use. It has had nearly twenty years of use and at this point the heating element and the turning handle have problems. The worry now is to find someone capable of updating the facility.

There have also been improvements in the two older outdoor privies. Several years ago, a Bobcat was hired. Each of the existing outhouses were tilted up on end and the hole under each facility was deepened from one foot down to four feet. This greatly lessened the chore of tipping up the privies and shoveling out the accumulated waste every two or three years.

Riverfront Erosion Barriers (Brother Larry)

Living next to a tidal river is challenging. Some of the riverfront problems result from increasing layers of silt caused by flooding which makes the channel shallower. A continuous procession of ships, barges, and tugs and speeding private yachts result in considerable wave action which damages docking facilities. The wear and tear never ends.

There is continuous erosion of the river banks. Over the years the Hudson River has worn away several feet of river bank in spite of efforts to diminish the wearing process. I recall in my late teens covering a significant segment of the river bank with cement embedded with rock slabs. It was a demanding job and seemed to result in a sturdy structure that would last for decades. Within five years, cracks appeared in the cement and within a few years after that, the once sturdy barrier had disintegrated completely.

Brother Larry solved the problem by creating two huge erosion barriers which have lasted several decades. With his mechanical engineering knowledge, he designed two separate erosion barriers: a 20 foot square structure at the southern docking area and a truncated pier-like structure on the north end of the docking area which was completed in the late 1970s. Both of these projects involved huge expenditures of time and labor.

Navigation on the Hudson River is controlled by the Army Corps of Engineers, a federal agency. Their job is to keep the river free from navigational hazards, such as floating driftwood and rocky outcrops. Over the years, they have built miles and miles of dykes to prevent riverbank erosion. Their job also includes dredging in areas where the channel has become too shallow for shipping.

Since the Army Corps of Engineers is part of the federal government, its finances are controlled by the federal budget. What with worldwide military involvement as well as demanding social expenditures domestically, there is seldom enough budget money available for infrastructure upkeep which would include maintenance of the rivers and waterways.

And, even within the scope of such needs, there is competition among all of those waterways which have to be maintained. For instance, shifting shoals in the Mississippi present a constant hazard which demands funding by the Corps. Is that more important than our Hudson River problems?–the answer to that question has everything to do with the amount of political power in the hands of the Congressional members in the waterway districts.

When brother Larry drew up a proposal to construct two erosion barriers at the homestead property, he needed approval by the Army Corps of Engineers. Of course he encountered bureaucratic lag time but his projects were heartily endorsed by the Corps–since they were well-designed and would not require any federal funding assistance. A personal note from the local Corps administrator thanked Larry for his proposal and wryly suggested that he expand the project southward to the city of Hudson, some 30 miles downriver.

The erosion barrier at the southern docking area was the first to be constructed. Once again, the Port of Albany made sturdy but aging timbers available, since they were being discarded to make room for newer steel docking facilities. The heavy timbers were the framework for Larry's erosion barriers. To get them in place, people with cables holding the struts upright were stationed offshore in rowboats to jockey them into position. The barrier was about ten feet tall and twenty feet square. Once the imposing frame was in place, rocks and topsoil had to be carried in for fill.

Our only means for transporting the rocks which were gathered from the river shore was a 1930 stripped down Ford Model A doodlebug with a 4 foot square wooden bed built behind the driver's seat. Larry estimated that about 150 loads of rocks would do the trick. Since I and several of my young children were involved in much of the hauling, this estimate became our goal. But 150 loads? Would you believe that 350 was closer to the mark?

A second sizeable trapezoid-shaped barrier was constructed just north of the swimming area.

Special recognition must be given to Larry's most competent assistant, a young

Norwegian, Leif Hanken. Larry met Leif when his ship was anchored near Alesund, Norway during the early '70s oil crisis. They established a friendship after numerous social occasions which apparently involved a lot of drinking. Leif was in his 20s and not ready to settle down. They entered into a bargain whereby Leif would come to upstate New York and be Larry's assistant in a variety of construction projects. Leif would provide his talent and ambition and for that he would get lodging and some limited financial remuneration. It turned out to be a bargain for all of us. Leif had a keen sense of humor and an ability to charm just about anyone he met. He befriended our extended family and has remained a much-loved guest over several decades. He was also a reliable worker.

Eventually the erosion barrier projects were completed and, surprisingly, they are still effective after forty years of holding back the Hudson.

OTHER RIVERFRONT IMPROVEMENTS (JOINT FAMILY EFFORT)

As a family of avid swimmers, it was critical to have an area to access the Hudson. We were fortunate--at the north end of our riverfront property there was a beach some 200 feet long. Years ago it was sandy with just a few large rocks interspersed. The area was ideal for learning to swim and to enjoy *surfing* small waves coming in when the Hudson River Day Liner passed by.

When we grew older, however, a deeper-water access area became preferable for the seasoned swimmers who had outgrown the beach. In the early 1900s the Army Corps of Engineers had built a sturdy dyke of vertical logs with filled-in rocks. It was probably a follow up to the Staats Landing' area used as an access area for colonial ancestors arriving by boat and in more recent decades as a deep water access for barges arriving to fill up with ice from the ice house.

At any rate, we were blessed with a swimming area that was about 12 feet deep at high tide and 7 feet deep at low tide. This provided a fine location for a diving platform which morphed from a spindly 15 feet tall structure made from two by fours in the 1930s, to a sturdy 10 foot tall crib of heavy-duty railroad ties which was filled with rocks in the 1960s.

There was a good reason why a sturdy crib evolved. In the 1930's and '40s and early '50s, whatever had served as a diving platform had periodically been swept away by the powerful movement of the ice in the river, particularly in early spring.

The spindly two by four version had been built and rebuilt, and eventually it was replaced by a platform set atop metal barrel drums. That, too, was swept away by the ice. By the 1950s we had learned the lesson that a more permanent structure was needed.

Once Larry had completed the trapezoid-shaped erosion barrier at the north end of the deep water swimming area, it opened an opportunity to build a swimming area deck some twenty feet square which could also serve as a fine dance floor. That prospect appealed to our party loving family and in the late 1980s the deck, complete with access ramp and terrace made of pressure treated wood was put in place. It involved the help of family and friends over a period of several months, but was a most sturdy structure, once completed. Within a few years, however, it became obvious that the entire deck should have been at least 10 inches higher since the original one was under water at high tide. A replacement deck was built and has served well for at least 25 years.

THE GAZEBO (BROTHER BARRY)

Brother Barry came up with some terrific ideas in the late 1990s. He became a real visionary in terms of land use and development and had converted a few acres of brush-covered scrub land to beautiful lawn areas. The gazebo was a very welcomed addition to the riverfront area. A local carpenter and good friend spent the entire summer building an attractive gazebo measuring approximately 18 feet in length and 13 feet in width. It was built overlooking the swimming deck/dance floor and just south of Larry's erosion barrier. It has served as the perfect sitting area to enjoy breezes off the Hudson in warmer weather. A dozen metal rocking chairs provide gracious seating.

This is an ideal spot for relaxing with a small group of friends. It has also served as an altar for weddings and as a bandstand for numerous all-night dancing parties. Barry paid for more than half of the construction cost and the rest of the family paid the balance.

LAWNS (JOINT FAMILY EFFORT)

In the 1930s when I was very young, the homestead environs were most uninviting. We'd lost our dad and the seven offspring weren't old enough to keep the grounds in shape. Mother assiduously tended to her flower garden of marigolds, zinnias, morning glories, hollyhocks, tiger lilies and daisies but she had little time for other outside work—household chores were just too demanding. There wasn't a mowed lawn on the premises.

Then came our consuming interest in croquet.

The grass had to be trimmed so that the ball could roll easily from wicket to wicket. At first the game was played only by the older generation, but in short order it became a favorite past time for the younger set. From somewhere a reel-type lawnmower appeared and the croquet grounds on the knoll just east of the homestead became the favored playing area. Compared with today's lawn tractors, pushing the reel mower was a frustrating, time-consuming chore shared mainly by Brother Barry and I.

During World War II, an Englishman invented the fuel-powered rotary mower which initially used razor blades for cutting. That was a significant improvement over the reel-type and we readily changed over to the newer mower type.

Eventually, when Mom got to the point where she couldn't maintain the flower garden, we converted the area just south of the kitchen overlooking the river to lawns. Of course once the new lawn proved to be so attractive, the brush area between the house and the river, once occupied by the icehouse, was converted to a cultivated lawn. It looked wonderful.

Then Brother Barry started his quest for gracious lawns extending to four or five acres. At first, for mowing the outer areas, Brother Larry introduced us to his multi-purpose Gravely tractor. Later we abandoned that machine in favor of John Deere and Toro lawn tractors which are easy to run and take only a few hours a week during the warmer months. The lawns are now beautifully maintained and, in recent years, we have even decreased the amount of acreage cut; particularly those areas than cannot be seen from the homestead.

THE RIVER WATER PUMPING SYSTEM (JOINT FAMILY EFFORT)

Since the homestead was built, the only source of water was a dry well dug some 30 feet deep approximately 300 feet south of the homestead. Occasionally, the water supply from the fresh water well would dwindle and concerns would arise. The only option was to transport in water from an outside source, such as a neighbor's well or the super market.

Larry decided to address the water supply problem by designing a system of pumping water directly from the Hudson River. This water would be used for gardening, car and boat washing, and would significantly reduce reliance on the fresh water well.

Trenching 900 feet of soil about 3 feet deep was undertaken and several of us bent to the task. It took several weeks, but when finished, there were six faucet outlets from which river water could be drawn. Three outlets were available near the house itself, while three others were located on the lower lawns and outbuilding areas.

Keeping the water pump running was a chore in which Larry took pride. He was a mechanical and electrical whiz and constantly tinkered to ensure proper pressure and preventing stoppages was in his line of expertise. And, of course, the pump had to be drained in wintertime to prevent freezing.

After Larry passed on, the task of keeping the river water pump system operational became a sporadic endeavor. One adept nephew was very mechanically talented, but lived more than fifty miles away. He came up with the idea, however, of buying a much lighter-weight pump that could be removed and stored in a sheltered location during the cold weather months. In recent years, daughter Giss has tackled the pumping problems and there has been significant improvement in the availability of river water in the summertime.

Roofing Concerns (Joint Family Effort)

With the homestead standing nearly 320 years, there has had to be continuous attention given to the roof(s). I understand the original roof was gambrel style but there was a serious fire centuries ago and the gambrel roof was replaced with a standard sloped roof. In the 20th century the main roof was covered with zinc-based tin shingles. There are four other roofs to be maintained. On the north wing of the house, brother Barry, the sole owner, maintained the tin shingles but the lower roofs were covered with rubber—which has held up remarkably well.

In the older fieldstone section of the house, there are two lower small porch roofs sheltering entrance-ways, and a much larger L-shaped roof protecting the veranda on the south and west sides of the house.

Depending on finances, ambition, and choice, the lower roofs have seen different coverings over the years. At one time it was tarpaper but more recently cedar shakes have made the lower roofs more attractive.

While the main roof covering the original fieldstone section of the house was made of tin shingles, the western wing of the house, added in the late 19th century, had a flat tarpaper roof. This required constant maintenance because of annual leaking problems. Brother Barry would spend a good part of his summer vacation doing the tar work, and it wasn't fun.

The main roof, which was of zinc-plated tin shingles, required fresh paint every four years. If we waited until a fifth year, rust would develop on the outer edges of the tin shingles. For decades we adhered to the dreaded four-year cycle of painting. Usually Barry did half and I would pitch in on the other half. I hated it. Often friends or other family would mount the ladder straddling the roof in order to help but no matter how the job was allocated, it became a chore.

Once in a while, a distraction would make the painting job even more loathsome. I recall being up on the roof at mid-day with the sun glaring down unmercifully when I heard the damned telephone ring down in the kitchen. This was in the day before cell phones, so to answer I had to get down off the roof. I let the damned phone ring. And it rang, and it rang, and it rang–twenty-three times! Thinking that such extended ringing mighty signify an emergency, I finally gave in and climbed down off the roof. When I got to the phone, I heard the voice of a dear old lady from church whose message was anything but urgent. It was exasperating and when she discovered what I had to get through to answer the phone, she apologized sweetly. She closed with, "Oh, dear, now you can go back to your fun up on the roof!"

In recent years finding help had become more of a challenge–the younger generation are off to college and/or working full time summer jobs.

In 2012, the fourth year in the cycle approached. After much haggling, the shareholders decided it was time for a new roof–stainless steel sheets guaranteed to last 40 years without painting. Amazing! Each shareholder pitched in about $500 and we hired a 6-person crew who replaced the roof in three days. With a little luck, we won't have to worry about the roof for some time.

OTHER IMPROVEMENTS

Back in the '40s brother Kim's north wing became his sole jurisdiction and the living quarters were spare to say the least. There was no running water, central heating, plumbing, or electrical service. Kim bought a generator to solve his electrical problems. In the meantime he used his basic knowledge of electricity to wire the north wing up to code at that time.

In addition, Kim hired a handyman to pickaxe a trench a few hundred feet long leading from the fresh water well to the house. A water pump was installed in a cistern and we had cold water service to both the original fieldstone section of the house as well as to the north wing.

In later years, a full scale heating system, including hot water tanks, was installed at the first floor level of the north wing,

Brother Larry incorporated a 15-gallon hot water heating tank in the kitchen of the old section of the homestead so that sufficient hot water would be available for cooking, dishwashing, sponge bathing, etc. An inside lavatory and a central heating system remain to be installed sometime in the future.

Brother Larry, a bachelor merchant seaman, sailed often as Chief Engineering officer on ships and oil tankers. He would sail for several months of the year but would take lengthy respites to spend time at home. He lived in the old fieldstone section of the homestead under very Spartan conditions–no central heating, indoor lavatory, etc. Wood stoves heated the kitchen and the living room fireplace was the heat source for the main living area.

Over time he laboriously installed the electric wiring system throughout the house. Some would say he overdid it, but we sure appreciate the multiple electrical outlets and those helpful lights which turn on when a closet door is opened. There was also generous outdoor lighting available which is so welcome on those winter nights when darkness closes in early. The outdoor electrical system is also useful for late evening and all-night parties.

As she patiently awaited electrical installation, my mom soldiered on and we got through WW11 with kerosene lamps and a battery-operated radio.

SWIMMING

Even play times involved physical exercise. Softball, swimming, ice skating, and sledding–all kept the blood in circulation. By far, my favorite physical exercise was swimming—I began at about age four and have been at it ever since.

There is no physical exercise that compares to swimming. On a warm inviting day, immerse yourself in the cool water and relax. I am often asked about being afraid of exhaustion when swimming long distances. *Nonsense! Take your time–go easy. Doing a casual breast stroke is never exhausting and it gets you where you want to go in whatever time it takes.*

In the Upper Hudson River there are tides, but they never flow at challenging speeds–and even when there are faster moving currents one can roll with it. For instance, when swimming across the river during an ebbing tide it is quite possible that the other side will be reached a few hundred feet south of the spot where you entered the water. You compensate for that by, before starting the return swim, walking north along the other side until you are a few hundred feet north of where you started on the other side.

Rip tides are reportedly a fearsome ordeal. The best advice is not to fight the current but instead swim with it until it subsides and then swim ashore when there is a lull. I was told this by an Australian with a great deal of experience. Right away, as I listened, the vision of sharks entered my head.

"But what do you do if a shark appears while you are casually swimming with the rip tide?' His reply, "Now you have brought up an entirely different problem." He abruptly dropped the topic of conversation at that time.

Lately, in these advanced years, I find it worthwhile to keep track of my exercising by counting each *bicycle pump* of my right leg in the water as I simultaneously do the breast stroke. It seems this literally becomes a double form of exercise—doing the knee pumps simultaneously with each arc of the outstretched arms. The whole body benefits–and as an accounting enthusiast it even means exercising the brain as you count.

We lived on the banks of the Hudson and in the warm weather months the river was always there for relief. The Hudson was very polluted back in the 1940s and '50s and '60s. Tugs and barges would pump their bilge water into the river. Cities and manufacturers had open sewer lines leading to the Hudson. Masses of oil slicks and grease were ubiquitous. In the spring, chemicals from a Rensselaer dye-making plant killed spawning herring–so much so that the river would be covered with thousands upon thousands of floating dead fish. In later years, chemical pollutants such as PCB's were dumped into the Hudson by the General Electric Corporation. And all this time farmers were having their fields sprayed with deadly DDT, which of course eventually found its way down through the soil and into the water table.

In 1965, there was an anti-pollution bill passed by the New York state legislature which mandated that all municipalities and corporations dumping waste into the Hudson had to build filtration plants. For some time, there was measurable and visible improvement. Blue crabs appeared in the waters for the first time. There was much less debris. By the 21st century, however, many polluters have outgrown their filtration facilities. During heavy storms drainage pipes overflow into the river.

In recent years there has been significant action by an environmental group, the *Riverkeeper*, founded by the Hudson River Fisherman's Association in 1966. The waters are patrolled and tested and reports are issued periodically. This past summer, the area by Staats Island was graded satisfactory for swimming.

The Staats family and friends have continued swimming. The river was right at our doorstep and too inviting to resist. In our youth we played water tag hour after hour. When teenagers, we tried out water skis, knee boards, and plastic tubes or even rubber tubes from truck tires. If an oil spill became a threat, we would block it from getting into our swimming area by tying a log out perpendicular to the riverfront dock.

I recall a summer visit by a sharp-witted teaching colleague. We were observing my children swimming in the Hudson. "You know, Bill," he suggested, "you should enter the children in the Olympics swim race competition. If they can swim this fast in water this thick, I'm sure they'd be guaranteed to win."

Diving was challenging and brother Larry was excellent at it. The swan dive and the jackknife were variations he mastered.

Swimming season started about mid-May and lasted through September. It seems part of each day was spent swimming. For me, swimming underwater was an enjoyable challenge-for which I once won an award at a church summer camp.

The family was so addicted to swimming that the younger ones were taught at the early ages of 4 and 5. Son Grant tailored swimming into a career, rising to the rank of Captain with the Navy SEALS.

I never enjoyed salt water swimming because of the sticky sensation on my skin after leaving the ocean. Pools are fun but confining. Nothing could compare with the Hudson, except perhaps mountain lakes and streams. In recent years, when arthritis invaded my hips and knees and spine, I would go to the local Senior Citizens Center where there is a huge pool. Unfortunately the walking distance between the parking lot and the indoor pool is just too much further than I can deal with. When booked at a motel, I always insist on staying in a room near the pool. Still, nothing compares with the river.

It has been a family tradition to swim across the Hudson and back at least once a summer. The width of the river is about 1/4 of a mile and it takes about 45 minutes each way. There have been occasions when there were 20 of us making the trip. We have a couple of boats accompanying us in case of problems and also to signal other river traffic that the swimming fete is on. In recent years, moreover, it seems some of us are lucky enough to stay agile into advanced age. I made the swim at age 83, but must admit to feeling very tired toward the end of the return lap. It will probably be best to call it a day although the challenge is still alluring.

In recent years when grand offspring and their friends visit, it pleases me to see so many plunge into the Hudson without hesitation.

On Being Very Clever

It isn't in my nature to be clever. Never mentally quick on the draw, either. I'm the kind of guy who will get into an argument one day and think of a great rebuttal several days later. So I surprised myself by exhibiting special acumen one summer. Perhaps it was because I had been goaded into a state of rage by an outboard motor mechanic.

In early June one summer my Suzuki outboard engine developed a problem and so I towed it on a trailer to an outboard motor mechanic who specialized in repairing that type of engine. He seemed like a friendly and capable guy and I left his shop with the guarantee that the engine would be repaired within a week. He also estimated the repair cost to be about $500.

A week later I phoned to see if I could pick up my motor. "I'm having a little trouble getting the part I need," he responded. Those things happen now and then so I wasn't overly perturbed. The following week I phoned and received the same answer. By now it was a few weeks into the summer season and I still had no use of my boat. I wasn't happy. I wrote him a firm note requesting that he immediately contact his supplier or find a replacement part.

I called again the third week. The part hadn't yet come in, "but it's due in a day or so," he guaranteed me by phone. By now I was steaming! I wrote him another letter–this one much more of a scorcher than the first. And so it went on throughout the summer–delay upon delay. Phone call after phone call, letter after letter.

I found out the name of the outboard motor parts dealer in New Jersey and gave him a call. You can imagine my chagrin when the dealer told me the part had been in stock all summer long!

I gave the mechanic one last call, lambasting him for his incompetence.

Two weeks later, he called me. Cheerily he announced that the Suzuki was repaired and that I could pick it up any time. By now the summer boating season had drawn to a close. I don't recall ever before being so upset with a tradesman. Not only was the boat late, but the cost of the repair had escalated to $1,200!

My cleverly devised plan was to give the guy $300 in cash and the remaining $900 balance by check. I calculated that the cash would serve as bait to seal the transaction. With that I drove to the repair shop, paid the $300 in cash, and towed the trailer and motor off the premise sand immediately drove to my bank where I stopped payment on the freshly written $900 check.

For some reason I didn't hear from the guy for three weeks—when he finally phoned to say, "Mr. Staats, it seems for some reason that the check you gave me bounced." I gleefully assured him that the cancelation was deliberate and added: "Please take the matter to court—I have written evidence of my attempts to get the job done—and I hope you land a judge who owns a boat and would recognize your incompetence."

I never heard from him after that.

ON BEING NOT SO CLEVER–THE LOST BATTLE

Rather than revel in my clever actions as in the preceding incident involving the stop-payment check, there are those memorable situations which I recall with embarrassment. For instance, not that long ago I went shopping at one of the nearby supermarkets. I selected a grocery cart and proceeded to walk along an aisle, dropping my purchases in the cart. It was after a few selections that I observed an older woman who was behind me also dropping her selections into my cart.

"Excuse me, but you are putting your groceries in my cart," I politely reminded her.

"This isn't your cart; it's my cart" she replied.

"No, it's mine," I voiced, tugging on the cart.

"Get your hands off my cart," she snarled, firmly gripping the other end of the cart and pulling it away from me.

A real tussle ensued. A young store employee tried to intervene, but the tug of war became more intense. Neither of us old-timers was willing to give ground. Other customers' heads turned to catch the confrontation.

After several yanks by each of us, my opponent threw up her hands

"Keep the damned cart. You're much older than I am and you're an old fool" she said walking away with a friend to find another cart.

I went on with my shopping spree but came to an abrupt stop when I spied ahead of me an unattended cart, partially filled with the things I'd been purchasing. The old lady was right. I was claiming her cart. My face flushed with embarrassment. Spying my contender and her friend in a nearby aisle, I walked over and meekly whispered into the ear of her friend, "She was really right and I apologize." I didn't have the guts to own up to it to the dear old soul and apologize.

Eight

SPIRITUALITY

For me, every step of the way in the process of aging and maturing has been influenced by spirituality. I consider spirituality to be a private matter and seldom discuss it outside of my family. Starting in my teens, religious convictions grew and became more deeply imbedded as the years passed. This all began formally with weeks of preparation in church sessions in my early teens.

I try to live my life adhering to the Ten Commandments and truly believe in life hereafter. For almost all of my life I have been very involved with the First Church in Albany (Dutch Reformed) and spent forty years as treasurer and as a member of the choir. I love the aura, personal friends, the sermons and the music. There is definitely a void when I miss a Sunday service.

Some of my family, like many others in the younger generations, don't get involved in church.

This doesn't bother me because, judging those closest to me, they still adhere to moral values. Somehow they just don't want to get involved in organized religion and I personally think they are missing some wonderful opportunities for meeting people, cultural improvement and the exhilaration of joint worship.

Nine

I have been blessed with a most enjoyable life. Receiving blessings throughout life suggests that they are bestowed on a special kind of person–*which I am not*! While I thoroughly appreciate the turns in the road that my life has taken, I take little responsibility and remain in wonder as to why I have received so much grace.

Tracing developments since the very beginning of 1932 has been an inspirational pastime. There have been so many changes of pace which could be accounted for in a number of ways. Many, many decisions have been made, usually with little regard to their overall effect on the long run. Were these *wise* decisions really a matter of wisdom? I don't think so because in the early years, there hadn't been enough experience to develop a framework for processing a pattern of reaction In later years, wisdom may have played a role, but I'm not so sure courses of action were that well thought out.

Luck? Luck suggests chance and I never thought of the vicissitudes of life being something of a whim. When it comes to those areas where luck could have played a major roll, as in gambling, it hasn't been all that kind to me.

In my younger years, I played poker with friends– never for more than pennies and usually as a social pastime. I was invariably *unlucky* and very seldom came out the winner. This was also true of the New York State Lottery. I began buying scratch-offs and lottery tickets some forty years ago when I wanted money to finance a second trip to Australia.

Playing the lottery became a habit and it went on and on since 1976. I just was never *lucky* except in only one or two instances. As an accountant, I assiduously kept track of my winnings and losings and patiently waited and hoped for the *big win* which never came. To make the process a little more exciting, I would buy scratch-offs and tickets on a regular basis but only check them out at the end of the month. I even kept slips of paper with my tally of wins and losses on a monthly basis.

Analyzing the results, I came to the conclusion that on the average, I was winning back only 1/3 of the money handed out. Only on a few occasions did my monthly intake come close to what I have spent. Obviously, luck wasn't on my side as far as the lottery was concerned. Surely, wisdom could in no way be involved if I lost consistently, month after month and year after year for forty years. It is embarrassing to learn that some $40,000 has been wasted in the pursuit of a lucky win.

A third destructive interest, casino gambling, consumed me for about twenty years. My wife loved it and had considerable luck. I didn't. Yet the glitter and ambiance were hard to resist. Time after time I lost–and yet I kept going back! Oh yes, I would set a limit for losing to about $150 a casino visit, but was always tempted to exceed that limit once caught up in the action. I lost at casinos across the country and even internationally!

Finally, in the past year or so, I came to my senses. I just wasn't lucky at gambling and there was no wisdom at all in continuing the pursuit of a never-to-be-reached goal.

So I quit–almost cold turkey.

Now I seldom buy a lottery ticket or scratch-off and I keep my casino visits down to social occasions enjoyed only two or three times a year. Why I didn't come to my senses decades ago, I'll never know. But at last, wisdom prevailed and my main regret is in not recognizing the stupidity of my actions much earlier in life.

But I am philosophical about the gambling. I've convinced myself that if I hadn't gambled, I probably would have diverted my financial resources to something equally expensive like chancy investments or a costly hobby.

I do not put much credence in happenstance. Things don't just happen for no reason. I'd much rather be guided by faith and grace.

There's also been another potentially dangerous habit which has been kept under control. It was the consumption of alcohol. I really enjoy a drink or several, and this could have led to dire consequences. After I reached drinking age, the gates opened and I was always ready for a fun time. The Navy experience only further whetted my appetite for grog and certainly the college years until marriage were replete with memorably joyful alcoholic outings. My marriage took place in 1957, but that in no way slowed the social whirl.

There was one controlling factor, however. My wife, Sandy, was no teetotaler but she kept a concerned eye on the amount of alcohol we enjoyed. At an early state in our marriage, we would have one or two martinis before dinner. That had the effect of lightening our spirits, but it also resulted in a hazy aura night after night. After several months of tippling before dinner, we gave it up. Having young children coupled with numerous other responsibilities ruled out spending evenings in a haze. Now, I have to ask: was it just luck that we decided to cut back on the booze? Surely there was an element of wisdom–but I still believe it was the *grace* of the Lord that gave us the impetus to curtail the heavy drinking.

Experiences attributed to good luck have been rare and most of my *wise* decisions were based on well-thought-out consequences, such as that time when I rescued my outboard motor from an unreliable mechanic.

I've ruled out good luck and wisdom as the most powerful guiding influences in my life. That leaves grace, and my appreciation for it will never diminish. In overwhelming balance, mine has been a good life and I just don't think it has much to do with my innate ability. I think it has everything to do with grace.

Over eighty years ago, I was born in very abject circumstances–my dad had died as a result of an accident and the family faced a future of poverty and maybe even splitting up and going to foster homes. To make matters worse, it was in the early years of the Great Depression so the entire economic outlook was dismal. This could have led to disastrous future. But some force brought Uncle Wil into our family life and we all survived to become a strong family who remained loving and in close contact. This was a force over which I had no control and yet it was to my benefit. Why me? I can only feel that grace had everything to do with it.

And so I spent my early years with a loving family, caring teachers and the double advantage of both city and rural living experiences. In spite of so few material perks, mine was a happy, enriched childhood. For Christmas, we expected little-but that was the way it was. My siblings and I had Christmas stocking filled with nuts and tangerines. The gifts were usually needed clothing–mittens, socks and underwear. For entertainment, there was usually a coloring book and crayons or a parlor game.

Once in a while, an unusual Christmas gift would make its appearance. Brother Bleecker received a much-wanted air rifle–and later in the day shot every ornament off the Christmas tree. Needless to say, Christmas or no Christmas, he got a spanking.

After Christmas, brother Bleeck would immediately start harping that the next family celebration of the year would be his birthday on March 8. Over and over and over he would dwell on the forthcoming event. Since my birthday was New Year's Day, there was little celebration because the excitement of Christmas was still fresh.

Naturally, I was a little resentful that Bleeck would take the limelight. As the youngest, I was spoiled and a real pain in the butt about it at times. I remember one of Bleeck's early birthdays when I put up a terrible fuss because he received a *Snow White* coloring book and I got nothing. Why should I have? It wasn't my birthday and I was just being a spoiled brat. But by golly, it paid off. I was given the same kind of coloring book just to shut me up.

The next milestone in my life was the accident where I was severely burned on November 7, 1939. The results could have been a disaster. I could have died or have been disfigured for life. But along came Dr. Harold Browne and the experimental plastic surgery which, at no cost, was miraculously successful. And what control did I have over that? There was no wisdom and I wouldn't attribute it to luck. It had to be the grace of God.

In World War II, our family suffered no serious losses. Luck? I just don't think so.

My high school experience from 1946-50 was idyllic. There were caring teachers and scores of close friends. My academic progress was above average. While no sportsman, I was asked to be the scorekeeper for the basketball team. In addition, there was the fun of singing in the high school chorus.

We were assigned to the same homeroom teacher for the duration of our high school experience. My teacher was much like a den mother and she nurtured a group of some thirty who weren't disruptive and who thoroughly enjoyed each other's company. As a matter of fact, several of my entire graduating class remained in contact for decades after leaving school. I had at least a dozen friends who would be considered close friends for life. Some might say I was lucky to have had such a great four years. I can't agree. It certainly wasn't due to wisdom, either. I can only thank God and his grace.

Throughout all of this, my mother was a rock who provided continuous guidance. She had led a difficult life, but in later years, we all matured enough to show appreciation for her efforts. Was I lucky to have such a great mother?–some people would say that, but I think there is more to it than luck.

Was it good luck that I briefly attended the Coast Guard Academy and decided it was the wrong future for me? I don't think so, but I do know that I was happy to work toward a most satisfying teaching career.

In the middle of my college career, the Korean War prompted my decision to temporarily leave home and join the Navy. My life there was enriched by meeting friends from across the nation, by getting in some travel and, along the way, experiencing the independence of being away from home. Don't ask me why I chose the Navy experience, but I know it wasn't luck. The war demanded my involvement and *someone* determined which choice to make.

In the mid-1950s I met the sister of a very close friend. In later months, the friend married and both his sister and I were wedding attendants. After that I asked her out. Our first date was a horseback riding expedition which we both enjoyed. For two years, we spent practically all of our free time together and late

1956 we decided to get married. I couldn't have made a better choice. Was it luck? I just don't believe it was just happenstance–some form of guidance from above prompted my decision to marry Sandy.

My next stroke of good fortune was finding a teaching job at Hudson High School. How was I to know that many of the small high school faculty would become intimate friends–and why did it just so happen that the secondary school principal was an exemplary administrator who always backed his faculty in public—but counseled better handling of problems in a private conversation. For four years, I enjoyed the high school teaching experience, but must admit to often becoming impatient with the immaturity of my students. I believe there was some wisdom involved in choosing to move on to the community college level of teaching, but there was also an undeniable degree of grace on the part of a guiding influence.

I started my high school teaching career within three months of getting married. While at the secondary school, my two oldest boys were born, followed by five more children in the years to come. Having a relatively large family was evidence of even more grace. The children were an endless source of joy for Sandy and I and, though challenging and expensive, we would never have done differently. Just watching them mature and make their way through life has been a comforting experience. And the best part is that we all remained friends right into their adult lives. Somehow, it seems they have become even more caring and loving as the years passed. Now that's grace!

Teaching at the community college for nearly 50 years was terrific. The students were fun to be with while also maintaining academic competence. Many of them became lifelong friends. My faculty colleagues were good friends at work and socially, too. Even those administrators that I came to be friends with became lifelong companions. More evidence of grace.

The sojourn to Australia and teaching at the Royal Melbourne Institute of Technology (RMIT) was one of the most refreshing changes of pace imaginable, and in spite of the financial strain and the often damp and chilly Melbourne weather, Sandy supported the year away from home wholeheartedly while managing a family of five small children. The year in Melbourne enabled us to experience some interesting travel, different dining options and, best of all, cementing friendships with people on the opposite side of the globe. These are friendships which have lasted decades! I don't think the decision to take on such a dramatic change in our life could be attributed to luck or wisdom. I'll ever be grateful for the guidance.

How do I account for the decision to shift emphasis in my teaching area from manual accounting to computer software while computer knowledge was still in its infancy? Whatever impelled me to make such a change which would rapidly change the entire accounting world? It was grace, I'm sure.

The retirement years have been very kind to me. For the main part, good health has prevailed. I've had opportunities to enjoy even more travel. Best of all is the evolving of even closer relationships with my family. They have been there when needed, particularly in that period following the passing of my wife.

My son Greg looked after me for ten years. After he died, my family and I got together to develop a plan whereby daughter Vicky would move into the upstairs area of my town house. We wrote an agreement about future ownership and distributed it among our immediate family—this well-thought-out action was surely prompted by grace with a touch of wisdom.

Ten

HEALTH WARNING INDICATORS

The unexpected anxiety of reaching age 83 came over me, quite suddenly it seemed, when I awakened one morning. The long-term mental and physical aftereffects, however, arrived incrementally a few months later and have been in play ever since.

Throughout life, I seldom had problems sleeping. There was the occasional anxiety spell or depression but those passed with hardly any notice. They would result in a lackluster day after with no lasting effects. I suspect that my lifetime of physical and mental activity were the reason for easy sleeping.

It was six months after the anxiety attack when noticeable change gradually occurred. More and more frequently there were nights when concerns about absolutely nothing of importance would cause so much tension that sleep was difficult. Breathing became more of a problem. It occasionally became difficult to catch a deep breath. These difficulties were often accompanied by hours of lying awake worrying about such mundane concerns as: Was there enough wood in storage to last through the winter, or concerns about the hordes of persecuted Burmese who had been on the evening news, or unfounded uneasiness about relationships between relatives.

These bouts with anxiety would usually start in the middle of the night. Dealing with them was frustrating. I employed different tactics–changing sleeping positions–sitting up and breathing deeply for lengthy intervals–opening a book and reading–sipping water—sleeping pills. There were times when a tactic worked and times when it didn't, so an array of differing methods were employed to combat anxiety and sleeplessness.

These periods of restless nights would last for weeks at a time and then there would be a respite for a week or so.

In the summertime I would sleep at the homestead in the used pop-up trailer which I had purchased ten or so years previously. It was a great experience sleeping in a protected area out of doors. No mosquitos or worries about furry intruders. The main problem was leaky canvass roofing. Ah, but there was a way to avoid that. In the warm months the pontoon party boat no longer had to be under cover and was rolled out from under the metal carport brother Barry had bought to protect his party boat from the winter weather. With the area under the carport area free, the popup trailer was parked under the shelter for the summer months. When the rains came, it was comforting to lie inside the popup listening to the soothing patter on the carport roof overhead.

The big advantages of sleeping in the popup were the view and the cross breezes. With the canvass flaps unzipped there was a panoramic view of the Hudson. This was particularly compelling in the dead of night when passing ships and tugboats cruised down the river. Even on the muggiest of nights, the popup was cooled by slight breezes coming from various directions.

Another of the popup's advantages for me was the ability to have an escape when a party was going on nearer the homestead area. It was always enjoyable to be with friends and relatives during daytime activities and occasionally there was the additional camaraderie around an evening outdoor fire. With the advanced years and the need for more rest, it didn't disrupt anything if I abandoned the group and found my way to the popup for early bedtime.

With reluctance on my part, summertime at the homestead drew to a close as the cooler weather arrived. We had a very warm autumn, which was a blessing. Nevertheless, the more confining life at the town house was not as enjoyable.

The sleeplessness problem continued. Just when things seemed unendurable, however, there would be periods of complete rest which, of course, caused me to think that the anxieties were in the past. Then there would be another night of unnecessary apprehension over some unresolvable problems and the sleeplessness cycle would restart.

In mid-October I developed a mild cough which would not go away after several days regardless of preventative action taken. It was about then that an unexpected change in medical care became available. More grace. Blue Shield hospitalization was starting an experimental program whereby seniors with several health problems would be eligible for house calls by physicians and other support medical personnel. That was an offer that seemed almost to be too good to be true.

The visiting doctor was a godsend. She could administer medical expertise in the form of taking my temperature and blood pressure and even take blood samples. She would write prescriptions. She was available to make house calls whenever needed and, most importantly, was cheerful, competent and friendly.

The consistent cough morphed into bronchitis and then to borderline pneumonia. The inability of my system to get rid of the fluid building up in my lungs had everything to do with my anxieties which were caused by breathing difficulties. Antibiotics provided a temporary cure.

By late autumn, the breathing problems had passed and I began to seriously consider repeating the annual change of pace which I'd enjoyed for several years. To avoid the hazards of winter walking and the boredom of February, I had taken to driving for several weeks in the south.

This year's itinerary began with a stopover at my daughter Heather's home in late January. Driving to her residence north of Philadelphia took about four hours. The family visit and overnight stay took me on the first step of the itinerary.

The following morning, Heather and I drove west to Harrisburg, PA, for lunch with former teaching colleagues who had moved to the area to help care for their grandchildren. Often, my daughter Heather, who was a real estate agent and who could budget her time accordingly, would accompany me. She preferred to drive and I thoroughly enjoyed being a passenger, so things worked out for the main part. I say *for the main part* because there were some aspects of the adventure that were unsettling. Heather has a heavy foot for the accelerator–often hurtling us along at 80 mph. Couple that with a proclivity for texting while driving, and you have the *perfect storm* for trepidation. And, too, there was the blaring disco music from the 70s. Nevertheless, I thoroughly enjoyed the conversation, reading the map, and viewing the landscape.

We would next make a motel stopover in Raleigh, NC, to spend time with my grandson, his wife, and my two great grandchildren. We treated them to dinner which gave us a chance to enjoy the newest additions to the family.

A few hours further south we made a two-night stop-over in Charleston, SC, to spend time with a grandson attending college there. Charleston is a beautiful city with some most interesting sites. The historic section is especially interesting when viewed from a ride on a horse and carriage rental.

From there, Heather and I parted company. I proceeded southward in my car, and Heather's plans were to either drive a rental car or fly back home to the Philadelphia area.

In the past, I would deliberately stop over for a night on the outskirts of Savannah, one of my favorite cities. It was always a treat to take a leisurely drive through downtown, seeing the gracious homes and hidden gardens and the myriads of small parks. The main thoroughfare is lined with huge trees festooned with Spanish moss. The cobblestone roadway along the Savannah riverfront has some unique seafood restaurants.

This year I bypassed Savannah and headed directly to Daytona Beach, Florida, where I overnighted in a mobile home park with my niece, Judy, who was wintering there from upstate New York. Since this was my first night without Heather, I didn't trust myself alone at a motel. Not only was Judy great company, but she'd had the experience of caring for her invalid husband for several years before he passed away. I knew she was adept with (a) old people, (b) wheelchairs, and (c) endless patience. We had the good fortune to have dinner at a local seafood restaurant, Aunty's Catfish, an outstandingly popular attraction.

After a leisurely drive south along route A1A, I arrived at Vero Beach, the home of one of my closest friends for more than 60 years, Ronnie Currier, who married my best high school buddy, Bob. For twelve years, she looked after Bob at home as Alzheimer's ravaged him. His passing in no way diminished my relationship with Ronnie. She had moved south several years previously so that Bob could take walks during the cold winter months. She, too, owned a home in a mobile home park—which featured one of the finest outdoor swimming pools I'd ever enjoyed.

While it was terrific sharing time with Ronnie, my ambulatory disability was becoming more of a problem. It was necessary for me to support myself with a rolling walker that I had stored in the car. The trouble was, neither Ronnie nor I, being similar in age, had the strength to get the damned walker in and out of the car. It was then that I concluded that I needed stronger and younger assistance for the rest of trip. I stayed with Ronnie for three overnights. Trouble sleeping and breathing once again became an annoyance. To make matters worse, the weather for southern Florida was inhospitable with winds, rain, and unseasonably low temperatures in the forties.

From Ronnie's I phoned Torill, my retired sister-in-law in upstate New York, asking her to fly south and join me, expenses paid, for the remainder of my driving trip in the South. She agreed to come within a few days' time.

I had considered visiting Anne Kirsch who also lived in another mobile home park, but demurred reasoning that Anne, too, was nearing my age and how unfair it would be to ask her for physical assistance in getting around.

My next stopover in Florida was two overnights in North Port. An old college friend, Ray Call, was wintering there and it was terrific to touch base with him. Not only that, he was in fine physical shape and handled my wheelchair with agility. We had two great days together, having time to relive our earlier years together. His wife had recently died after decades fighting Parkinson's and this was an occasion to spend happier times together.

Next, I scheduled a three-day visit with friends who owned a condo in Naples. My sister-in-law, Torill, arrived by plane. We had a terrific time with the couple who had also shared some years with us decades ago when they rented the north wing of the homestead in their earlier honeymoon years. The Fallons are interesting, ebullient, and most hospitable. Time raced by. Persistently in the background, however, I had breathing problems accompanied by impaired sleeping efforts.

A few miles from the Fallon's condo, I had arranged to rent two rooms at a luxurious resort for three days. My daughter Heather and her husband, Don, took time to stay at the hotel-where I could get a significant discount because of a long-time friend in upper management of the Seattle-based hotel chain. While in the Naples area, the weather changed to sunshine and temps in the 80's for those days.

From the Naples area, Torill and I drove north stopping over at a motel and then spent the next night in Destin, FL, where we enjoyed a terrific evening with my grandson Evan, now in training with the Navy.

From Destin our intention was to start the return drive home and we made it as far as 20 miles south of Atlanta, GA. It was there that my breathing difficulties became unbearable. We had stopped at a motel with a swimming pool and I took a swim. At this point my breathing was belabored and had diminished to small gulps accompanied by pains in my lower left side. It was so bad that I avoided swimming to the deep end of the pool for fear of not being able to support myself by treading water.

When I got back to the room, things became increasingly worrisome. I just didn't have the strength to get fully dressed and could only put on my briefs and socks. Torill suggested that we call an ambulance and I heartily agreed. This was more than we could handle alone. In a short time, I was in the ER at Piedmont/ Lafayette Hospital. They gave me an IV and within an hour my breathing was back to normal and the pain had subsided. For two overnights I stayed at that hospital. The care from all of the staff was excellent.

My daughters Giss and Heather flew to Atlanta. I was released from the hospital and Heather and I took a flight to her home area of Philadelphia and the following day, she drove me back home. Giss drove my car from Atlanta to Albany, and Torill also took an Albany flight. At last, I was on home turf but feeling apprehensive about the future.

At that point my offspring, particularly Vicky, stepped in and began managing my recuperation. Doctor appointments were scheduled. An oxygen machine was brought into my town house. Tests and medications were prescribed. What a relief! Vicky had me on a rigid schedule. The other offspring stopped in for regular visits and sometimes prepared the evening meal for me to eat at home. Once again, I was blessed.

It seemed to take me a long time to find out the exact cause of my breathing problem–which was congestive heart failure. I had been blaming it on sleeplessness which was really only a symptom. My heart specialist explained it this way: For most people, advanced years are accompanied by diminishing heart strength. At the peak of most lives, the heart performs at 60% of its ability. (Smoking, improper diet, and/or lack of exercise are why it seldom performs at 100%). My heart is currently performing at 35%. The heart pumps out body fluids that accumulate in your lungs. If the heart isn't strong enough to pump out the lungs, these fluids accumulate and cause problems with breathing, coughing, sleeping, etc. One way to ameliorate the problem is to take water pills which eliminate the body fluids— DO NOT, however, decrease water intake because it could negatively affect the kidneys and liver.

Another source of health benefit is to be connected with an auxiliary source of oxygen which strengthens both your heart and lungs. The pills, the nebulizer and the oxygen seem to be working for me. I only need the oxygen during the nighttime, which gives me considerable freedom during the day.

Eleven

CONCLUSIONS

Does the foregoing information summarize *all* of the lifetime effects which might have caused the sudden anxiety of reaching my 83rd birthday? Probably not. I do, however, think I have included the most important influences: (1) world events (2) family, (3) health (4) social life (5) education/career/travel (6) physical accomplishments (7) spirituality. Some of the above have diminished in relevance over the years while others seem to be playing an increasingly important role in terms of influencing my prospects for the future.

WORLD EVENTS still interest me, but not with the enthusiasm I had in years past.

EXTENDED FAMILY has become even more important as time goes by. Having seven thoughtful, caring, and ever-present children was, I think, the biggest blessing of my life. Add to that so many other terrific relatives and close friends. They're attentive to my health needs, stop by often to visit, invite me to dinner and other social events, keep me up to date on developments, etc. Life would be so empty without them.

HEALTH issues are a continuing annoyance but it is important to realize that things could be so much worse. Arthritis in the knees, hips and spine is physically painful while continuous bladder distress is more of an annoyance. And then, of course are the usual aging problems with hearing, sight, and teeth. Added to all of that are concerns about diabetes, blood pressure, kidney and liver problems and even dermatology. Golly, gee, but aging is fun!!

SOCIAL LIFE has diminished significantly because so many of my friends have passed away or have moved out of the area. In addition, the inability to get around without discomfort has limited my horizons. It is critical, however, to keep these friendships going as long as possible. Scheduling lunch or visits has been a source of satisfaction. I have had to withdraw from many church activities and other organizational participation.

EDUCATION/CAREER/TRAVEL have diminished in importance to me as the years have passed. At one time, they were among the main focuses of my life and they have contributed immeasurably to my current bank of fine memories and my outlook for the future.

PHYSICAL ACCOMPLISHMENTS are a source of both pride and frustration. Pride in that I achieved so much at a time when I had the ambition and capability—frustration with the realization that I can no longer get involved in physical activity. Just about every day I encounter a problem which I could have previously taken care of with ease—but now have to defer to others for help or simply accept the fact that it will have to wait until sometime in the future—or perhaps not get resolved at all.

SPIRITUALITY has had an increasingly positive influence over my negative attitudes. When there is a relapse into temporary depression, meditation and prayer play an uplifting role.

Narrowing down the main causes of sudden anxiety upon reaching the 83rd, I would cite health concerns, diminishing social contacts, and frustration over physical limitations.

GRACE, WISDOM, AND LUCK have seemed to stay with me as continuous companions. Grace from God has always been there and wisdom has accumulated over the years. Often enough, luck—or was it wisdom--will also evidence itself, such as when, in my most recent physical crisis, I had my sister-in-law with me. If it hadn't been for Torill, I probably would not have made it to the hospital in time.

Twelve

WHERE TO GO FROM HERE

C ongestive heart failure has placed undeniable limitations on my activity. What should be done in the
light of these recent signs of physical deterioration?

At this stage, my most lingering health fears are
(1) being incapacitated by a stroke or (2) by breaking bones as a result of falling. There's a limit to how
much prevention can take place other than attention

319

to life style and careful movement. Slipping on the ice or tripping over an obstacle are the usual causes of concern and even extreme caution doesn't always guarantee safety. Like everyone else my age, the hope is to pass away quietly while in dreamland.

There is an up-side to all of this gloomy speculation—the prospect of death simply doesn't worry me. I have lived a terrific life with an amazing amount of blessings. While I will miss my family and friends, there is another world out there that might hold some wonderful experiences. There are so many people I hope to see when I get there. So many for whom I am grateful to have had in my life before passing on–my wife, my mother, my siblings, my son, Uncle Will and hundreds of others.

I am apprehensive about the physical pain of passing, but I am sure that concern is shared by everyone else.

The present, for me, is frustrating. Not to be able to engage in physical activities I most enjoy, such as walking, travel, and working on the homestead, is discouraging. And I don't see any improvement on the horizon. Nor should I after all of these terrific years. At times, it doesn't seem there is much to look forward to–but that is an ungrateful attitude after receiving a lifetime of blessings.

There is yet another up side. My mental faculties are still sharp! It's great to be able to enjoy doing those things of which I am still capable. I can still become immersed in reading good books or enjoying a fine meal, or doing a challenging crossword puzzle, or playing a parlor game–or even soaking up the warmth of a radiant sun. Driving and swimming are still favored pastimes. Social contacts remain invaluable.

Some in my stage of life would consider self-termination and I must admit to occasionally harboring those thoughts. If a health situation results in severely diminished enjoyment, why go on? From what I read, however, the results of this action can lead to devastating effects on loved ones. This, once again, stresses how influential family and friends are both during your lifetime and beyond.

I have told so many people that if I ever decided to do myself in, I already had a plan. I would choose a frigid February night, venture out into the cornfield nearby the homestead with a bottle of really fine vodka, lie down on a blanket and take several swigs followed by a long, endless sleep.

So much for negative thinking!

The sensible option is to take each day as it comes and continuously strive to be upbeat and appreciative of those things to be grateful for. It is so easy to wallow in self pity, but that leads to depression which makes you someone to be avoided.

I'd like to share some advice to anyone with similar circumstances to mine:

Preparing for the future beyond death is critical. It's just not fair to leave others in a quandary due to neglecting to straighten out one's personal affairs before dying. A power of attorney and an executor and a health proxy should be assigned. A Life Sustaining Treatment and/or Do Not Resuscitate Order should be considered. Funeral arrangements should be attended to as should drawing a will. If it can be done without creating a maelstrom, will preferences should be explained and in writing. I have notified my offspring of my preferences—even to the extent of asking them to select any of my possessions they would like to have after my passing.

In maintaining social contacts, I find it isn't enough to just wait for someone to stop by or call. Those contacts are appreciated but if they don't occur, then take action to make them happen. Accept invitations to dinner; take the initiative by phoning a friend and asking them for lunch or invite them to your home for a visit. If you can't attend an event, thank the host for inviting you and ask them to remember you the next time around.

Take physical care of yourself as much as you can. Meet doctor appointments and follow a schedule of taking medications. One of the reasons I found myself in that hospital near Atlanta is that I failed to use my nebulizer (inhaler), even though my daughter had packed it in my car. Even when breathing became more and more belabored, I continued to ignore the nebulizer. How stupid was that?

Increase your reading, if that is an interest. You don't have to be ambulatory to pass time with a good book. Keep up any enthusiasm you have for music or sports or any other special interests. Television is another possibility, even though much of it may seem a waste of time.

There is now abundant time for reflecting on the positive aspects of the past as well as prayer and meditation. And along with all of that—rest–it's good for you.

65483989R00188

Made in the USA
Middletown, DE
27 February 2018